Annie

Where Did the Sunshine Go?

Donna Forster

◆ FriesenPress

Suite 300 - 990 Fort St
Victoria, BC, V8V 3K2
Canada

www.friesenpress.com

*This book is loosely based on true people and real events. Names have
been changed, any similarity to real people is strictly coincidental.*

ISBN
978-1-03-910511-9 (Hardcover)
978-1-03-910510-2 (Paperback)
978-1-03-910512-6 (eBook)

1. BIOGRAPHY & AUTOBIOGRAPHY, PERSONAL MEMOIRS

Distributed to the trade by The Ingram Book Company

Table of Contents

Prologue

I wrote this story in memory of a young woman in the sex trade whom I met and got to know well. It is loosely based on her journey.

I pray that this book helps bring people an understanding of the many women and men caught up in the sex trade. How at times they end in the snares of addiction.

Donna

Thoughts

I wander through life, hoping for something. I'm not sure what. Maybe my life is like mist—part truth and part fiction.

My story is real, but part of me wishes it is simply mist that will disappear when the sun starts shining.

I seek the mist, lest the truth destroy me.

I have a place I hide, in my mind that is soft.

Pink and blue clouds keep me warm, and, above all, I am safe.

There are no others in this place, and no one can hurt me here. I can make the rocks soft and my wishes attainable.

I can fly on wings of angels, dance among the stars, and drink wine from the big dipper. There is no one here to see or hear my tears falling.

I can love me and feel valued and, above all, wanted.

Yesterday cannot come here, but I ache and welcome tomorrow, hoping tomorrow brings promise.

My story is about flesh, blood, and bone. It is not a new story; it's an ugly story that should never be allowed to happen. I am not alone in my story. There are many like me.

We have wishes, but no dreams—the nightmares will not tolerate them.

You look but you don't see me. I am a ghost with skin.

June 30, 2015

I can hear them screaming and swearing as I approach the corner. I know Sissy, who is a regular and this has been her corner for a lot of years. As I draw closer, the other woman quickly retreats.

"What in the world is going on?" I ask Sissy.

"I dunno who she is, but she was working my corner!" She is angry, and tears well up in her eyes.

"Everyone knows this is my corner—who does she think she is comin' down here and taking over my territory? I otta rip her hair out. She's lucky she ran, or I would have messed her face really good so no one would pick her—not tonight and not for weeks."

Sissy paces back and forth, her anger spewing words out of her that don't bear repeating.

"Settle down Sissy. She's gone; the corner is yours." I walk away and follow the direction I saw the woman run, hoping I can find her.

I spot her a few blocks away.

Annie

This street is very dark and lonely. She is standing on the corner, in front of a building that has three steps, which the women often sit on when their feet get tired, or they want to visit with each other on a slow night. I have never seen her before, and I am curious and worried at the same time. She is petite and very, cute. She is wearing white shorts and a cute pink halter top. She has beige sandals with thin straps, which are decorated with multicoloured beads across her foot, no ankle straps. Her hair is dark and mid-length, worn in a bun with a riot of little curls squeezing out. She tries to cover the escapees with a beaded headband the colour of her top. Very chic look about her. I guess her age to be around 26-plus. She doesn't look like she belongs here.

I approach in a way that she can see me coming and I try to ensure I don't appear as a threat.

"Hi, my name's Donna, I come down to these streets every Thursday night and give out a little bag that contains candy and a pass it on card with a message. I have never seen you before. I slowly ease closer to her and try to ask her questions in a way as not to appear like I am cross-examining her.

Are you a local worker, or are you working a set route of several different cities and towns? Are you part of a stable, or are you independent? Is this your first night here?"

She looks like a deer caught in headlights.

"My name is Annie and I just moved to here. This is my first night out here and I thought that crazy woman was going to kill me!" She blurts.

"Yes, that was quite a tantrum, but Sissy has worked that corner for a long time, and it was quite a shock for her to see you working it when she came to start work. You can relax, she has settled down. You will like her when you get to know her. I smile at her and invite her to sit on the steps and try to relax. Where are you from?" I ask, taking a small step toward her.

"Prince Albert."

I can see I am going to have to pull every bit of information out of her. She steps back from me and I sense her discomfort and fear. She takes a couple of steps back and I wonder if she is going to bolt again. I stand very still making no moves toward or back. I maintain eye contact and I try again.

"I have been coming here once a week for more than 20 years. It is a ministry that I do. I belong to a church that prays for me and supports me. Have a look inside this little bag. As you can see, it has some candy, a small bottle of body spray, and the card has a picture of a little boy saying to his crying friend, "Don't worry about tomorrow, God is already there." It is one of my favorite pass-it-on cards. I hope you will accept this little gift. I mean you no harm, I promise."

She looks at me and bursts into tears. I take her hand and we sit down on the cold concrete steps. My heart hurts for her. I wait for her to tell me how she came to be working these streets.

I believe her tears are a result of the onslaught she got from Sissy. At the same time, she is faced with me and my questions. She does seem to sense that I am not here to hurt her.

She gulps in some air and tells me how she ended up here. "I drove my two little children here to start a new life. I haven't been able to get any work and we desperately need help. My family are all in Prince Albert, so I am all alone." The tears leak in profusion with this statement. I had to leave Reenie, my best friend in the world. We could talk about most things openly. We have always been there for each other since grade school. I miss her so. I have met Sarah, my neighbor. She's great but I can't tell her my heart secrets like I could with Reenie. Phoning her is not the same; it's just not. We have no furniture and little food. I have spent most of the money I had."

She sobs openly now, wretched desperate sobs, exposing her depth of helplessness. She puts both arms over her forehead and onto her lap.

"Hey Annie, you are not alone anymore. We can help you. How old are your children?" I ease my arm across her back.

She swallows her sobs and jerkily tells me. "My daughter is four and my son is two." She looks up at me, the little bit of mascara she wore is now marching unevenly down her cheeks. The shock of her encounter with Missy and my efforts to help have done a number on her. She looks thrashed and so darn sad.

I stroke her back trying to soothe her. "Who is with them right now?" I pray she has not left them alone, as some of the women do when they are working into the morning hours.

Her sobs have quietened, and she is more constrained now. "My neighbor across from me," I silently say a quick prayer of thanks. "We trade off babysitting. She watches Micah and Jessie while I look for work and now at night. I take care of her little boy, Jamie, while she is working. She works days, so I am trying to get a night job. My best friend in Prince Albert suggested I try this as she works every now and again. She says it is pretty safe provided, I stand on a corner that has a streetlamp and some steady traffic. She told me it has been a lifesaver for her when finances got really, tight. I thought I would try it. It seemed exciting until that girl went ape on me and chased me down the street." She is annoyed now and put out.

I chuckle to myself at her indignity. "I will put a call out tomorrow and see if we can get you some furniture; it won't be new, but it will work for now. Are you sure you want to do this Annie?" Working as a sex trade worker is not like what you might read in books. It is not like being married, where you have a say in what you want. The guy who picks you up will negotiate a fee, but he will dictate what he wants from you. You cannot always get away from them unharmed if you do not agree to their terms. Did your friend explain any of the guidelines women have embraced as safety precautions?" I hesitantly ask.

"Not really, but I plan to be very, careful before I get into a car. I know it's not like being married. I'm not reckless, and I'm pretty good at taking care of me. I don't need some stranger telling me what to do. I know what I need to do. I'm not some young kid who might just jump in a car without asking a few common-sense questions. At this point, I just need to look after my kids and keep them safe and well fed. Please just leave me alone!" Her back is up, and she is offended.

I have invaded her space now and I need to back off. "OK, but just a couple of quick suggestions: the first thing you should know is that these corners are like territories. Some of these women have been working their corners for a few years and won't accept anyone coming along and taking it over." I pause and smile. "You learned that lesson the hard way tonight. This corner is not taken, as the woman who worked it has just left and started a course at Camosun College. The second and last thing I will suggest is you don't allow anyone to go bareback—always insist they use a condom. It is a good idea for you to always carry a good supply to ensure you are protected. Before I leave, just so you know, in that little bag I gave you ... on the back of the pass-it-on card is my phone number and name. I am available 24 hours a day. I promise you, if you call me, I will do whatever I can to help you. Please trust me with your phone number so if I get some furnishings for you, I can get in touch with you. I will not share any of your personal information."

I am surprised and relieved as she tells me her phone number. I type it into my contacts, and I thank her.

"I need to connect with Bess on another corner now, but please let me help you Annie, you can trust me. God is beside you even if you don't feel His Love for you. I promise you are not alone."

I walk away and head for another corner to talk to Bess. It is a busy night. I give and receive lots of hugs as I pass out my little bags. How blessed I am by this ministry! I leave for home around 11:30 p.m. I pray that Annie gets in touch with me.

July 1, 2015

The morning is lovely and warm, blue skies smiling down on me. I think of Annie as I eat my breakfast. I really hope she will call me. I wonder at her courage, driving all the way from Prince Albert, Saskatchewan to Victoria, British Columbia, with her two small children. She doesn't have family or friends here. I believe there is more to her story. I wonder if her husband is who she is running from or if it's something else.

I phone my church and ask my pastor to put out a call for any furniture, particularly beds, tables, chairs, a couch, dishes, cutlery, pots, and pans—any household stuff they can spare. If I get too much, I will pass it on to another woman who I know can use it.

I work 20 hours a week, four days a week, but not weekends. My shifts are done by 12:30 p.m. I leave for work and pray there will be some messages for me, about the furniture for Annie.

I love my job and my shifts go very quickly. I work in the most, friendly, coffee shop in an outdoor setting that is breathtakingly beautiful. Even on the busiest of days there is a sense of peace that embraces me, because of the natural joy that comes from the surroundings.

On my journey home, my thoughts go back to Annie. I wonder if there will be any response to my callout to my church. I have frequently stepped into these scenarios and, many times my church family has stepped into the fray and responded in a positive way. For me, the key to being able to reach out to help Annie is whether she will accept. Just as I start to get engrossed in these thoughts, a great song I love to sing to comes on my car radio. I burst into song, dance in place and enjoy my drive home. As I pull into my garage, I see Gipp out in the front yard, picking some very colourful flowers. I am humbled when he comes and hands them to me as I get out of my car.

Gipp, my husband, is a pastor and the best partner someone like me can have. He is supportive of the ministry I do and never loses patience when I get caught up in situations like the one which I am about to embark on. He had a counseling session with one of his congregants, booked this morning. I assume it went well. As we walk into our home, I hear the answering machine recording. I hope it is Annie.

I make each of us a cup of tea and a sandwich and sit down to listen to the messages. Praise God, there are numerous items of furniture, dishes, etc. being offered by many of our church goers. Some even offer to move the bigger items to Annie's home. I eagerly dial the number she gave to me last night.

The phone rings and rings until I am instructed to leave a message. I do that, remembering Annie told me that she cares for her neighbor's son during the day, along with her own two children.

I leave my message and ask her to call me as soon as she gets it.

I phone back everyone who has offered something and plan for most of it to be dropped off at my home. I ask those who are giving the couch and the bed to hold off until I check to see if Annie is willing to have them dropped off by them. I still hope a table and chairs will come forth, but I am happy about the wonderful response so far.

Thankfully, Annie does return my call, and we arrange for a group to help deliver all the stuff to her home. She is beyond happy at such a quick and great response.

I decide for us all to meet at my place, pack up the stuff and go to her home as a group. Three of the women offer to make sandwiches, veggies, and coffee.

The day we deliver the furnishings is overwhelming, not just for Annie and her two little children but for all of us.

Judy and Carol, a couple of the women quickly take charge of Annie's astonished children. Judy kneels in front of Micah and gathers him in her arms. "Oh, aren't you the cutest! She laughs as Micah nestles his curly head against her neck. He has light brown curly hair, intense blue eyes shielded by very, long eyelashes. He is wearing a light blue t-shirt with a white shaggy dog painted on the front of it and a tiny pair of jeans. His runners are blue with red lights that flash on and off as he walks. She gives him a lip-smacking kiss on the top of his head and takes him to a corner that has some blocks and other toys.

Carol gingerly approaches and kneels in front of Annie's four-year-old girl. She is little with big brown eyes and a riot of dark curls just like her mother, crowding her little head. They are corralled with a pink hair ribbon. Her dress is pink with white-and-yellow small flowers dancing all over it. She is wearing white sandals and her little toenails are painted pink. "Hi sweetie, what's your name?" Judy reaches and gently holds both of her small hands. "Jessie", she whispers. She shifts her little feet and sways from side to side. Her head is bowed, and she shyly peeks at Carol. "I have a pretty bow in my hair, my mommy put it in to make me look pretty." She murmurs. "I know, I see it and it is very pretty and you are even prettier." She hugs the little girl to her, and Jessie puts her arms up and Judy lifts her. Jessie lays her head on Judy's shoulder. "Oh, I love this." Judy caresses Jessie's hair. Let's go and play with Micah, is that okay with you Jessie?" "Uh huh."

There are many of us, unpacking and moving stuff from cars and trucks! We run back and forth for a good half hour just getting the items into the apartment. We shift furniture around when one of us decides that is not where they believe it should be. In the end Annie will make that decision and I assume she will shift some of the pieces where she wants, after we leave. Even the dishes will probably be rearranged. I know when I move, I always end up shifting dishes and utensils as I use them, for more efficiency.

What a great day we have, unpacking the dishes and arranging furniture. We stop briefly and sit around the boxes and furniture and enjoy the food, fun, and friendship while we eat lunch and drink coffee. A few hours later, we have made some semblance of order. We shifted most of the furniture around, and put the dishes, pots, pans, and cutlery into the spaces Annie chose for now.

We leave and I am pleased with what we accomplished today. Annie's apartment is a cozy one. She has many colourful pictures on her walls and now, with the furnishings and some pretty knickknacks paired with some lovely curtains that she said she had sewn together when Sarah loaned her a sewing machine. She shyly, showed us a throw rug she is making for her entranceway. Pretty pillowcases cover her and her children's throw pillows on the beds. It all adds to the warm, lived-in look created. It feels like a happy place when you walk in.

I hope she believes she can trust me enough to talk to me and let me help in any way I can. I know my church will be there with prayers and open arms welcoming her and her babies.

July 9, 2015

The following week I go to the stroll, which is in the downtown area, to chat with the women and search for Annie. I have been here for a couple of hours when I finally spot her on a different corner. This street is better, there are more lights and more women nearer to where Annie works. There is a covered entrance with a couple of steps on a building near this corner. I try to remember if anyone extensively uses it as her territory. I can't think of anyone and I am certain that Annie will be able to claim it as her own if she continues to work here.

As I approach, Annie sees me and gives me a huge smile. She has a sweet look about her. She is wearing a light blue short sleeved blouse and dark blue cargo shorts with black flip flops that are decorated with a white daisy. She has a dusting of makeup on, just enough lip gloss and a touch of pink on her cheeks, light gray eye shadow and dark mascara. Her dark curls dance loosely under a blue headband that is decorated with white daisies.

"Hi, Annie. How is it going?" I smile back and ease in front of her and I offer her one of my gift bags.

She accepts my little gift and does a little two step. "I am really excited my apartment looks nice and I feel settled. I am grateful to everyone who came with stuff for me. It was great how so many from your church came to help a person they had never met. I even got some table and chairs from one of the ladies when she saw I had nowhere to sit except on the couch. I know I can do this now and make it work. I know I am not alone now."

Annie seems hyper and very animated—quite different from the woman she was last week.

"That's great, Annie. I hope you and I can become friends. I am here every week and available if you ever need or want to talk."

She hesitates. "I think I should let you know that I left my husband," I had to get away from him because he was doing drugs around our kids and I was so afraid he would hurt one of us. He is quick to lash out when he is coming down from a high and needs more drugs. He spends most of his money on drugs and booze. I had to get as far away from him as I could. I knew Victoria was a long, long, way and the weather is so much nicer here. I wait each morning for the sun to start shining and am so happy for each new day. I am afraid of that lifestyle. I was even starting to smoke some weed with him, so I could cope." She looks astonished that she would do such a thing.

"Oh, Annie, I am sorry you had to make such drastic move. What about your family? Couldn't they help you to find a safe place closer to them? At least you would have support close at hand." I wonder why she wouldn't seek their help.

She looks unhappy. "No, my family was disgusted with both of us and told me to straighten up or they would seek custody of my kids and that I would not even have visitation until I could prove to them that I am a fit mother. If they knew what I am doing to get money, they would do everything to get my kids. I know they would!" She looks frightened and panicked.

I hesitantly suggest. "Please be careful out here, Annie," I reply. "There are lots of drugs to be had and there is always a risk when you go off with a john. I will be out here every Thursday and I will look for you. If you can, keep this corner; it is not as dark and there are women on corners near to you. If possible, when you feel more comfortable and trust the others down here, you might want to have one of them work this corner with you. It is a good idea to have a friend working with you so each of you can note the time you leave on a date and that you do return within a set timeframe you have both agreed on. Think about it and I will see you next week."

"Thanks Donna; I will give it some thought. I don't know anyone out here right now, but I will try and make some friends. See you next week." She smiles and walks to the corner.

I am still uneasy about Annie's demeanor; I can't help thinking she might be taking this occupation and all it entails too lightly. I can only hope she is being cautious and alert when she is approached by a john and when she is on a "date." I tend to be paranoid about these women when they first start out. Bad dates, drugs, and alcohol can be a real danger out here. I've been out here so many years that at times I assume drugs and alcohol are often used to ease all the negative emotions mixed in when working the streets. I don't want to crowd Annie by being overprotective or invading her privacy, especially since she doesn't have family nearby. I promise myself to call Annie this week and see if she wants to go for coffee.

July 16, 2015

I can't believe how fast the week has gone. I tried to phone Annie a couple of times to no avail. I hope I see her tonight. I have a couple of calls to make, one to an escort agency to connect with one of the women who works there. It has been a slow week for her, and she needs some food for her children, Contrary to what many people believe, the sex trade can be a hand-to-mouth financial journey. Sometimes, but not always. Some Escort Agencies are businesses that offer sexual services as well as dating sites.

The day rushes by and it is time for me to get organized and get down to the streets. On my way to Annie's corner, I get involved with Casey, another sex worker who has a small child and needs some extra help. She is medium height, a little skinny. She has dark chin length hair and it always smells sweet and clean when I hug her. She has deep dark eyes and wears darker shades of eye shadow giving her an intense look. Tonight, she has on a pair of jean shorts and a white t-shirt with a huge sunflower emblazoned on the front. Flip flops on her feet. Casey has a tendency to flare quickly and spits out unkind words and words not worth repeating. Tonight, she is consumed by her anger at her child's father and expends way too much energy thinking of all the things she is going to say to him and maybe hurt him if she can ever get her hands on him.

I finally get her settled and arrange to meet her at my home on Saturday and get some help for her. These women often come to our home for counseling with Gipp, or just to have dinner and experience some normalcy in their lives. Gipp has been an ordained, street pastor for many years and is a pastor in a small church on Pender Island.

I finally get to Annie and I am grateful she is on her corner and not on a date. I am feeling a little weary after my encounter with Casey, and I plan to go home once I have met with Annie.

I cheerfully greet her. "Hi Annie, how is it going? How are those two, little ankle-biters of yours doing? I assume they are settled and happy to be here."

"Hi, Donna. They are great; we all sing our little chant in the morning: 'I see the sun, the shining sun, so warm and bright today. The sun always shines for us,'" she sings. "I am a little tired tonight, so hope I can go home early. I'm busy these days, making some rather good changes in my life is wearing on me." She seems a little droopy tonight, and I notice that her pupils are larger, and she seems a little unfocused.

"I hope you don't think I am overstepping here, but are you smoking weed or taking some hits?"

Her demeaner immediately changes and she growls, "You know Donna, this is not the easiest way to spend my evenings, I am using, smoking some weed to get me through each night I'm out here selling myself to some scumbag just so I can pay my bills and give my kids things they need. It's none of your concern. I'm grateful for all your help and support, but that doesn't give you the right to question how I deal with all of this." She waves her arms to encase the whole street.

I am offended at her nasty tone. "You're right, it is none of my business, but I am just trying to help you Annie. I don't want to see you lose your kids. If certain government agencies get wind of what you are doing, you could get on their radar. And if they find out you're using, you put yourself, and your kids right in their sights. They could take your kids from you and put them in the system: none of us wants that to happen. You're the best person and the one person they need in their lives right now. Just sayin' I'm not here to hassle you, but remember I am here to help, and part of that help includes my encouraging you to stay off any drugs, including marijuana. I'll see you next week. Stay safe out here," I say and then walk away.

Annie turns away and spots a car slowing down, she walks toward it.

* * *

I wait a couple of days and give Annie time to think about our Thursday night conversation. I contact her and arrange for her, Sarah, and I to have coffee at Annie's apartment the following week.

The three of us get together on Monday. It is a civic holiday, so both Annie and Sarah are off work. I finished my shift for today and am looking forward to our afternoon together. Our conversations start off with chatter about the children, how well they are all doing, and how wonderful it is they all get on so well together. Both Annie and Sarah interact with the three children each day they work.

"How do you like your location, Annie?" I ask. "Does it seem to be compatible for shopping, walking, and other things you need to do?"

"I love it here, Donna. I am really happy that Sarah and I have become such good friends, I want to thank you, Sarah, for being such a wonderful neighbor."

"Oh, I feel the same about you Annie," she replies. "I love where we live right now, but both Jim, and I hope to be able to buy a home within the next couple of years. I would love to have a yard we could put a swing set in and maybe a small patio where we could all gather for barbecues and family get-togethers. That's for the future and I know we will be able to that sooner than we at first thought, so I am happy to be where we are at this point in time." Sarah smiles as she relates her goals.

Turning to Annie, I smile. "How about you Annie? Do you have any long-term goals?"

Her eyes light up and she smiles. "Oh yes, I love taking pictures. I hope one day to be a photographer. It has always been what I wanted to do. I really hope one day it will happen," she says between taking sips of her coffee.

"What a great way to make a living!" I say. "Taking pictures can be so exciting and fun, sad sometimes too, but they capture so much if you are good at it. I'm not one for taking or keeping pictures. I love looking at photographs, but I have never been attached to them for any length of time. I love scenic pictures and animals and people, for me, the best are the ones others take." I laugh at myself, knowing how pathetic I am at it.

Annie becomes animated as she explains. "Oh, I love what I see when I am focusing on my subject, no matter what it is, it is like a story unfolding for me. I don't just see the main subject of my photo, but I can visualize the story around it and what I am trying to create for my audience. I know I am good at it because I did it before I got married and had children. Many of my friends asked me to do their weddings, their children's baptisms, birthday parties, and lots of other private and public events. One day, I hope to get back at it." We enjoy how she bubbles with excitement and passion.

I am amazed at learning this and seeing the joy it brings. "Annie, I hope you achieve your dream. You know you can—maybe not today nor tomorrow—but you can do it. We'll be here to soldier you on. I can hardly wait for the day."

Sarah squeaks when she looks at her watch. "Goodness! Look at the time. I've got to go and start supper Jim will be home shortly. Come on, Jamie, let's go. Thanks ladies, it has been fun. We need to do this again. See you tomorrow, Annie." Sarah smiles and hugs her.

"Yes, it is time for me to head home too, Annie. Thanks for a lovely afternoon. I will see you on Thursday night. Take care." I gather my purse and leave, feeling good about how the day went.

* * *

The streets are quiet this Thursday, so I enjoy my walk-about with the women. I learn more new and fun information from a couple of them. Hannah plans to open a day care in a couple of months. She has done so well over the past five years she has been out here. She now believes she has enough money to go forth with her dream. She has two little ones, a three-year-old girl, and a new baby boy. If I remember correctly, he is three months old.

Susie is now enrolled in a cooking course that includes cake designing. She has always wanted to be a baker and loves to decorate cakes and cupcakes. I hope she attains her goals one day. She is still working hard at staying sober. It is important for these women to have a goal and reach for it. I often whisper to them when they are weeping and crying out to me for help that they need to reach for the stars. No matter how far away their dream is, it is always within their reach if they want it badly enough. Often, their response to me is how hard it is, particularly if they have a drug or alcohol problem. I always assure them that together we can do anything, that we are never alone, and we are the ones standing in the way of change. It is truly startling when they succeed—they are so proud and happy. And I do a little dance and thank my God. On my way home, I help solve some minor issues at one of the agencies.

Tonight, we have a couple of police bulletins warning us of two men who set up meets, negotiate the deal, the woman fulfills her part of it and the dates refuse to pay. A couple of the women have been beaten up, so I stop and talk with each of them about what's happening. Some of them know those who were beaten, so they are apprehensive. One of the men is posing as a police officer, which is very frightening. I spend extra time suggesting they work in pairs, with one being a spotter, making a set time to be back, and taking a close look at the john, making sure he seems safe.

I make my last stop at Annie's corner.

"Hi Annie, how are you and your little ones?"

"We're doing OK; the kids have really settled in and are pretty happy and excited at having playmates and we live close to a park so we can go there pretty well every day."

Annie slurs some of her words.

I step back and feel sickened by what I see. "That's good to know. Kids are pretty, resilient. It's good they're so well adjusted, that's on you Annie. You're a sweet and loving mom and you're doing a great job of raising them. You seem a little down. Is everything else OK?" I am worried.

Annie shuffles from one foot to the other. She hesitates and seems to be thinking about what she wants to say. I guess I have made her uncomfortable.

Now, I am uncomfortable standing here waiting for her response. Finally, I jump in with a couple of more questions.

"Do you want to meet for coffee one day, or do you want to go somewhere now where we can talk? I assume you know about the bad dates?"

I see her shoulders relax and she finally responds.

She is making a good effort at controlling her speech. "Yeah, I heard about them. I am careful who I go with. I was doing good, but I just found out my husband has followed me and the kids here. He knows my cell number and keeps leaving messages for me to call him. He wants to see his kids. I was going to change my number, but I figured he would never find me here. He must have called Reenie, and she probably let him know, not thinking he would leave his job and follow me."

"Are you afraid of him, Annie?" I step back a little, so she doesn't feel crowded or threatened by my questions.

She is slow to answer, like she is thinking about what to tell me. "A little, he's never hurt any of us, but he gets pretty out of control when he runs out of weed. I can't believe he quit his job; he's been there for over 10 years. I don't know how he's going to get work here and how's he going to pay for his stuff." She yawns.

'If it's okay Annie, I'd like to make some suggestions that might help to protect you. Maybe he just took a leave of absence so he could see the kids. Maybe he plans to return to Prince Albert, after he's straightened things out with you. It's probably best if you meet him and find out what his plans are. Don't invite him to your home, meet him in a public place so you can control the conversation and try a find out as much as you can. You are probably going to have to let him see the children, so maybe set up a time in a park and plan a picnic so the kids are comfortable. The park gives them and their dad a place to run around and play and just have fun. They shouldn't feel any tension between you two, so try and keep it as normal for them as you can. Just some suggestions. Please don't think I am telling you what to do."

She yawns again and looks toward the road as a car goes by. "Yeah, I'll think about it. I'll call him and maybe we can just talk on the phone and I can try to set up a picnic date at the same time. Yeah, I'll try that, I feel better. Thanks, Donna. Oh, there's my pick-up. It's OK, I know him; he's one of my regulars. See ya next week," she says as she walks away.

"Yes, I'll see you next week. If you need anything, or need to talk, call me. Stay safe out here tonight," I call out to her, but she keeps going and climbs into the john's car.

I finish my visits with a couple of latecomers and head home.

August 20, 2015

I am genuinely concerned about Annie. I go to pick up the phone to call her and it rings at that precise moment. It is Annie.

"Hi Annie, I was just about to call you to see how things are going with you."

"Terrible," she moans, sounding agitated. "We met at the park as you suggested, and he was really, kind and considerate, so happy to see the children. He says he still loves me and wants to make a fresh start. He claims he is clean and has been now for six months. He seems contrite and serious about what he is saying. He has no place to live, he has been sleeping in shelters." She takes a breath and gets a little more control of her emotions. "He wants to save the money he'd spend on hotels to help pay for expenses by moving in with us. He says he has a job interview next week and appeared quite sure he would get it." She has a bit more control as she continues on. "I don't know what to do. He acts sincere and apologetic that we are in this situation and he is taking complete responsibility for it because of his past problems." She starts to lose control again. "What should I do?" She is gulping in air; she seems annoyed and sad at the same time.

"I'm coming over Annie, I'll be there in 15 minutes. Put the kettle on and we'll have some tea. Do you have your friend's little boy this morning?"

"No, she has my two children; I'm too upset to look after them. I won't go downtown tonight. I look a mess and need to think about what I am going to do, quickly." Her voice quavers as if she is about to cry.

"I'm leaving right now; do you have any cookies? I love cookies with tea," I tell her, trying to keep her calm.

"Yes, I have peanut butter ones."

"Perfect! I'm on my way."

* * *

It's gridlock as usual in my area so it takes more time than normal to get there. Why, when speed is of the essence, are we always caught up in situations we have no control over? I am cursing and so darn frustrated at the slow-moving cars and getting more agitated. I seem to hit every red light slowing me down even more. I frantically weave in and out of traffic. This is just like me to get myself in a tizzy, imagining all kinds of terrible things happening at Annie's. When I can't get to where the trouble is, I instantly become enraged and useless by the time I arrive at my destination. Then I almost always discover there was no need to panic.

I finally arrive and dash up to Annie's apartment and practically bang the door down as I pound on it.

"I am so sorry it took so long for me to get here; the traffic was brutal!" I blurt when she opens the door.

"For goodness sakes, Donna, sit down and breathe. There is no need to panic. I'm OK, I just get scared and anxious when I feel threatened when it comes to my kids."

Annie sits beside me on her couch, soothing me when I should be helping her. She leaves to get our tea and comes back with a tray laden with a teapot, cups, and a plate of cookies. What is the matter with me? Why do I let myself get into such a tizzy over matters in which I have no control? I am frustrated and angry with myself. It takes me a few minutes to chastise myself and finally be in a state to talk with Annie!

"OK, Annie Again, I am sorry I barged in here like an idiot. Tell me what's going on with you and your husband."

Stalling she nonchalantly says. "You take your tea black if I recall." She pours our tea and offers me a cookie.

Under her façade I see she is struggling to control her emotions.

She hesitantly explains. "He has no place to stay and he wants to move in with us, but I am not sure that's a good idea. He says he's clean and sober, but I don't know that for sure. I have met with him twice. Lenny has had a sweet disposition both times, and really seems to care about me and his kids. I'm afraid if I don't let him stay here, he will get back smoking weed and booze again," she says and brushes away some run-away tears.

"Your cookies are delicious." I take a drink of tea and think about what to say. "It is hard for me to even make suggestions never having met your husband. I am sorry to repeat myself but, my first thought is to assure you that it is not on you to keep him off drugs and alcohol, it is on him. I know there is professional help available to you. You could seek out a counsellor in family and children's department and ask them to work with both of you, ensuring that you and the children are kept safe."

She starts to whine "I don't want to do that. I don't want to involve anyone else. I don't think getting Children's services involved is necessary. I still love him, and my kids need their daddy to be here. He came all this way to be with us. I really want to help him, but I am afraid, not only what he might fall into but what I might do. I know he won't want me to work on the street and I know he'll be furious if he finds out what I have been doing." She wrings her hands and squirms and jumps up and starts pacing.

I see she has made up her mind to let him move in. Anything I say now is futile. "Annie, you are going to be the one to makes this decision. I worry that your emotions will override what you know you should do. You have been doing the best you can to support your children and pay all the bills each month. I would love to see you get out of working in the sex trade, but you need to make that decision based on your own feelings, not on what you think he might do. Frankly, it is none of his business! If you don't want to bring in professional help, then I suggest you meet with him several times to ensure he is doing what he can to get work and that he is, in fact, off all drugs."

Sighing she replies. "Yeah, I know you are right, Donna."

She looks deflated, but I am grateful she is not going to cave and let him move in right away. I hope she makes sure he is working and will help with expenses.

Annie slumps and sighs, she seems to have no energy left. "I will let him know we are OK on our own right now and that we can keep talking. I'll invite him to supper and make sure he and the kids get some time together. I don't intend to quit working, no matter what he thinks or says. I know you would like me to quit, but I can't right now and most of my friends now are the women I work with on the streets. They are very, kind and supportive; we are like sisters."

"OK, Annie. Let's leave it at that; please don't make any snap decisions. You know that if you let him move in you won't be able to get him out without a whole lot of turmoil for you and your little ones. Please be careful and promise me you'll keep in touch with me, not only on Thursday nights." I hug her and feel her shaking, the tension in her body is intense, I am concerned.

I pause before I speak. "Before I leave, Annie, will you get rid of all the weed you have and please stop smoking it. It is just one step away from moving on to more powerful opiates. If he does move in, if you are smoking weed it could give him an excuse to do the same. I know it is none of my business, however, I worry not only for you but for your children—they must be your prime concern. I'll get out of here now. Remember, I am a phone call away. I love you Annie; stay safe and take good care."

"I will, Donna. And I promise to get the stuff out of here. I'll see you downtown, and thanks Donna, I love you too."

August 23, 2015

I am so concerned about Annie that I call Jeremy, a pastor friend of mine, and ask for his advice. He tells me what I already know.

"Annie needs to sort out her feelings and make a decision with which she is comfortable. We know what we would do, but we have no emotional connection to her husband. We don't know how much fear she has. Her main concern seems to be for him and for their children. She will make that decision based on her own concerns for both. From what you have told me, I believe she is still in love with her husband and has little self-confidence in her ability to go it on her own. We only know what Annie has told you. We can't judge her husband based only what she has related to you. You need to step back when he does get involved and try and see for yourself if what she has said is factual. We know she has struggled with finances since she arrived in Victoria and she probably believes what he tells her and desperately wants to have him by her side and wants the children to have their father back."

I glance at my watch and am shocked to see the time. I am late leaving for the streets.

"Oh my gosh, Jeremy. I have to go right now. Thanks for your time, I really appreciate it. The ladies will be wondering where I am."

"OK," he says. "I hope I helped, but we both know in the end it won't matter what we think. Annie will do what she thinks is best for her. Emotions will win out in the end and we can only hope and pray it will work out for her and her children. You stay safe out there tonight and let me know how this gal does."

"Thanks, Jeremy. It always helps me to talk things out with you. Good night."

"See you soon. God be with You!"

I feel better having spoken with Jeremy. I know I can't force my ideas on Annie, she has to decide what is best for her. I'm pleased to hear him validate that. I am behind now, and I grab my supplies for the women and head downtown to do my street ministry.

* * *

"Hi Donna, you seem a little late tonight. Is everything all right?" Missy asks me.

"Yes, everything is fine. I was on the phone with my friend and time got away from me. How are you doing, Missy? Is everything good with you?" She looks sweet tonight. She has on white cutoffs with a red crop top. Her hair is tied into a ponytail and pulled through the gap in the back of her baseball cap.

She shrugs and smiles. "Oh, well, you know … life sucks but I'm doing OK. I have been busy tonight; I need rent money this week, but it looks like everything will work out. You know how it is: I go from month to month and I'm always happy when I can pay my bills."

"Yes, we all face the same devils each month, don't we? Like you, I am always grateful to my God for always being there and giving me the strength to go forward. I am very blessed to have such a good life."

She shrugs. "Yeah well, you got your God. I hope He is on my side, but I don't know all about that stuff. I know … I know you keep inviting me to come to your church with you, but I dunno, maybe one day … I need my sleep, don't you know? I work long hours, so it's hard to get up early in the morning. Maybe when I make my first million, you and I can get together with your God." Missy laughs as she walks down the stroll.

"You never know Missy; you just never know. See you next week. Stay safe. Remember that God loves you and so do I."

I chuckle as I walk away. I love knowing my God is probably chuckling too. I visit a few more ladies and I spot Annie on her corner talking to some guy. I never approach the ladies when they are talking to men. I walk around and visit with Trea. She is one of my favorite people. I think she is in her thirties. She is always smiling and happy to see me. She is head and shoulders taller than me. She always looks put together when she is here. Tonight, she has a pair of cropped black pants with a white tailored blouse cinched at the waist with a multicoloured belt of pastel shades. She is wearing a black pair of flipflops. She gets excited when she tells me of things her daughter does or says.

"Hi, Trea. How has your week gone?" She walks toward me smiling. "It's been a pretty good one, Donna. I am starting to move forward, and my daughter will graduate high school next year. I am proud of her; she works part time through the summer to help me with expenses. I am taking a psychology course online, which I know will help when I am out here helping other women. I have been clean and sober for over a year now. Each day is one day closer to my dream, Donna."

I know one day she will be off the streets and on a much better road. One day, she wants to work with the 'ladies of the night' (her terminology) and help them move on. I know in my heart she will do just that.

I am on my final walk around and I see that Annie is alone on the corner.

"Hi," I say as I walk up to her and give her a hug. "How are you doing tonight? It's a lovely, warm night, and it seems like it's been pretty busy."

She seems steady tonight. "I'm really good. I had another meeting with Lenny, and I am fairly, sure I'm going to let him come and live with me and the kids. He is being sweet, Donna, and he has a job in a fast-food place. The money's not great, but it will help until he gets a job doing what he does best."

I am relieved to hear that. "That's good news Annie. What is his trade?"

She is more animated now. "He's a mechanic and a really good one. He'll get a job doing that, I know he will. He makes good money doing it, too. I am excited Donna. The kids love him so much; he's been spending a lot of time with them. It's good to have him home, I haven't seen any sign he is on any drugs or drinking."

She grabs my hand and smiles. "I'm really happy Donna, I hope you agree with my decision. I might even be able to give up this job when he gets settled in a better paying job then I will be able to start some online photography courses." She clings to my hand.

"Annie, whatever you do, I will support your decision. I just want you and the children to be safe and happy. I don't know your husband, other than what you have told me. You are the only one who can decide what you believe is best for you. I am excited and pleased to see you so happy. You deserve it and a haven for your family. Please keep in touch with me. I worry if I don't hear from you." I give her a big hug and smile.

She seems anxious. She glances toward the traffic, I'll still be working for a while, Donna; I promise I will let you know how we are, and I'll always be honest with you. I have not smoked since last week, so we are both doing good. I'll see you next week. I have a date coming round; he has circled the block twice and I don't want to lose him, so can you and I say good night and I will see you next week."

"I'm out of here." I turn and get off the corner. I head home and I am happy that all seems well on the streets tonight.

September 9, 2015

The days pass quickly, and it seems as if Thursday is coming up faster than it should. It is already Tuesday and I still need to do up my little gift bags and sign the pass-it-on cards. I gather all my candies, lotions, and cards, and just as I sit to get it all into the bags, my phone rings.

"Hello." I hope my exasperation isn't reflected in my voice.

"Hello, is this Donna? a strange voice asks. I am certain I don't know her.

"Yes, it is. Who am I talking to? If you're one of those telemarketers, I don't need anything. I don't have time to talk right now; I am in the middle of something that needs my attention," I reply, rather agitated by the interruption.

"Please don't hang up, its Sarah Donna, Annie's friend, right across the hall. You and I met for coffee; I look after her children. I am very worried about her right now and I don't know what to do. I remember you telling us about what you do and how your church helped Annie, when she

43

first arrived in Victoria," she rambled on. I don't believe she even took a breath.

Warning bells go off in my head. "Whoa, whoa, I do remember you Sarah. What's going on with Annie?"

"It's Len, her husband. He's moved back in and I am really worried about it … at night when she goes to work, I know he is doing drugs. I smell the pot from my place. He yells at the kids and turns up the TV so loud, I am sure people walking outside can hear it blaring. I don't think he is working anymore. Annie came over in tears on Monday and told me he said he wasn't going back to that place; it is full of losers and the pay stinks.' She was pretty upset. I think she made a mistake letting him move in so soon. She should have made him find his own place for a couple of months, just to make sure he could help with the finances. Annie struggles to make ends meet as it is without him sponging off her. Oh, you probably think it is none of my business and I am just one of those nosy neighbors who like to gossip, but I'm not like that. I worry about Annie and the kids." She hardly pauses, her worry building as she speaks.

"OK, Sarah; I hear you. I don't know what I can do unless Annie comes to me herself. I am afraid if I step in before she acknowledges there is a problem she will shut down and then we will both be unable to help. Let's just see how it plays out in the next couple of weeks. She may come to me and ask for my advice. If that happens, then I can set up a meeting with her and her husband and maybe get some answers on what his plans are and how Annie and the children fit into his future. I know that is probably not the answer you are looking for. I hope you will keep in touch with me and I know you will keep your connection to Annie and be there as a support whenever she confides in you about all that is going on. I will talk with Annie Thursday night and, hopefully, if she is worried about how things are going with Len in her life, she will say something to me, we'll talk again very soon I promise. Please keep in touch."

Sarah agrees and promises to keep me informed. I hang up the phone.

I no longer have the motivation to put my stuff together for Thursday night. Instead, I go out and work in my garden and, before I know it, it is time to prepare something for supper. I sit back on my haunches and breathe in the fresh fall air and embrace the beauty of the late-blooming flowers. I love to garden. I am not great at it but my flowers bloom and the lettuce, peas, and tomatoes flourish. The other things, like cucumber, squash, and cabbage-like plants do not come to fruition under my not-so-green thumb. I stand up slowly and let my joints catch up before I move to put away my tools and go inside.

Gipp is ready for something to eat and asks, What's for dinner?"

"Not sure," I say. "We have some beef soup in the freezer I could thaw out and we still have some of those buns I baked yesterday, along with some apple pie. How does that sound?"

"Sounds great!" he says. Gipp is so gentle and easygoing. No matter what food I put in front of him, he is always grateful and compliments me. I know I am one lucky woman.

September 11, 2015

I am concerned about Annie, but I need to get those gift bags done today, the sooner the better for me but I still have tomorrow if I don't do it today. I tend to procrastinate at times. I have a nice easy day and decide to get a quick supper. Gipp is in Vancouver doing voiceovers. Gipp has an amazing soft, expressive voice that magically envelopes you with a sense of peace and love. He does these commercials for a tech company in Vancouver. He has won several awards for his works. He also has a partner, Dale, here in Victoria, and together they record Christmas CDS. Gipp writes all the dialogue and recites them, and Dale writes the music and does all the recording and tech stuff. I plan to read my book and go to bed. It is already 8 p.m. and I am tired. I fill my tub with bath salts and hot water and sink into the warmth before I get into bed.

As usual I wake up early. It took me a long time to get to sleep last night. I could not concentrate enough to read my book and tossed and turned worrying about Annie. I grab some coffee and go to work putting the gift bags together. I struggle with this part of my ministry. It is very, important that I do not cross the line with these women, if I jump in where I want to rather than wait for them to invite my opinion, I can lose their trust.

I have a busy day ahead of me. I am having coffee with my friend, Betty, and dinner with Vivian later. I put together the bags and everything that I am taking down to the streets tonight, tidy up the area, and get ready to leave for my coffee meet. Both these women help at all the dinners we do for the sex workers at Easter, Thanksgiving and Christmas. They have both conversed with and shared dinners with many of the women.

I spot Betty as soon as I enter the coffee shop. I love to spend time with her; she is such a good and kind friend. We tell each other everything. We order our coffees and I tell her about the situation with Annie.

"Wow!" Betty snickers. "You do get yourself in the middle of crappy situations with these gals don't you, you need to watch your step; you do not know this Len guy. You don't know what he is capable of. The fact that Annie felt she had to come all the way from Prince Albert to Victoria to get away from him tells me a whole lot about him and her situation. You might want to think about distancing yourself and keeping her home life at arm's-length from you." She raises her eyebrows and smiles.

I titter, "C'mon Betty, you know I try to keep my distance. I don't think it is a dangerous situation at this point. Annie and the children seem excited that he is here. I believe she will be able to control the situation, provided he stops smoking weed and gets a job. I worry that they may graduate from smoking to stronger drugs if they continue to have to face difficult financial scenarios. We shouldn't judge Len until we have met him and get to know him," I reply to my worried friend.

We get on to more pleasant subjects and agree to meet and go to a movie this weekend. We both hug and promise to call sealing the deal.

I clean up around my place and then head out to enjoy my dinner with Vivian. She is always happy and has lots of news about her new house on the mainland and how much she enjoys her garden and the small community in which she lives. By the time I get home, it is time to get ready to go down to the streets.

It seems a bit quiet tonight, but it is still early, and the night traffic is just beginning. I see Sunny, one of the women.

Waving, I approach her. "Hi, Sunny, how are you doing? Your baby must be growing and becoming more alert and fun to watch."

"Yeah, my little Susie is cute as a button and so active. She crawls around opens cupboards and gets into all sorts of mischief. She is starting to stand up more and tries to walk but usually topples over. She is seven months old, and I am amazed at how smart she is." Sunny is very animated as she tells me all about her baby.

"You are doing a great job with her, Sunny. Are you still studying to upgrade your education so you can get a nursing degree?"

"Yes, I am just about done, and I have my name on the wait list to get into Camosun's nursing program. I am excited. I have lots of support from the Province. I am on track to getting a grant to cover my expenses, as well as receiving help with daycare for Susie. Things are happening for us Donna, and they are all good. Who would have thought I would be clean and sober, a mom, and now studying to be a nurse? And it all happened in less than two years! She laughs, twirling around.

"Yes, Sunny. You must be immensely proud at how far you have come! I am proud of you. You go girl—and keep up the great way you are living your life. Have a good night and stay safe. I'll see you next week."

I hug her and walk down the street, where I spot Annie.

"Hi Annie, how's it going?" I ask, handing her a gift bag. She looks nice tonight and has a glow about her. Her outfit is cute: pale blue jeans that hug her legs, a white, long sleeve sweater with a brightly coloured vest, and black boots. She has a little tam perched on her head with her curls dancing around to cap off her look. What a difference in her demeanor.

"Really good, Donna. Len has moved in and it is nice to see the kids happy to have him with us. He plays with them and takes care of them at night so I can continue to work. I was pleasantly surprised when he agreed it is best for me to keep doing this until he gets a steadier job that pays more. He is even helping to get the meals. I ask him to stop smoking weed and he has not smoked any since he moved in. He is clean and sober, and I am proud of how much he has turned his life around." She smiles and appears to be happy with her decision to let him move in.

"That's so good, Annie. I am glad it is all turning out so well for you and your children. I hope you can soon stop working down here and spend the evenings together as a family. You are looking good! You have a good night, stay safe out here, and I'll see you next week."

I walk around and visit with the women out working tonight. Most seem pretty settled and calm. I head home around midnight, happy for them and always praying their lives will change so that they find a better way to make a living. I understand their needs and how and why they ended up down here. I am here to pass on the love of my Lord and not sit in judgment. I love them all with their varied and fantastic personalities and am so blessed by the love I get from each of them. We do all we can to help them move forward with the goal always to getting them off the streets.

I pass Annie as I am driving home. I wave at her and I start to think about how vibrant she is tonight, and I pray that her friend Sarah sees that joy and maybe won't judge Len quite so harshly. I worry, too, that she may be right about what Len is doing while Annie is working. All I can do is be there for them when and if she needs me.

I am exhausted when I get home and literally fall into bed and sleep like a baby until 7:30 the next morning.

September 26, 2015

I have a quiet week and Thursday is upon me already. I seem to spend my time in ways that keep me busy so that time seems to be my enemy and slips away from me.

As I am driving down to the streets, my mind goes to thoughts of Annie. I stop and speak with Missy and Trina and a few of the other girls working tonight. All seems to be OK. Trina had an incident with a bad date earlier, so when she told me about him, I persuaded her to call the police and get an alert out so other women would be forewarned to watch out for him. As it turns out, one of the women recognized him from when he stopped to pick her up. She ran away but got the license plate number and we just got word that the police picked him up. We can all hope the courts will put him away for a few years. They are such scumbags. When they get these women in their cars or in a remote place or low-level motel room, they beat on them and do outrageous things to them because the women are caught unaware. Trina is vulnerable because her drug habit causes her not to pay attention to what's around her or clues that her date may be abusive. At least we have one more creep off the stroll.

"Hi, Annie. How are you doing? I am taken aback when I see her swollen black eye and split lip. Whoa, what happened to you?"

She immediately touches her face and takes a step back. "It's nothing. I fell and banged my face on the cupboard as I fell." Her bottom lip trembles.

"It's not nothing, Annie. What's going on? Did your husband do this? Let's sit down on the steps and talk." I ease her over to the steps in front of a nearby building.

She sits down beside me, I reach for her hand, but she pulls away. "Yeah, but it was my fault. I was nagging him about getting a job. I know he's trying hard to find work, but he can't seem to get any jobs. I know he is frustrated and mad that he can't help more, but I can't support him and the kids on what I make. I'm worried I won't make the rent because it costs more for food and other things with him living with us. The kids love to have him around, though, and I don't want to stop that. He gets enraged whenever I say anything about how hard it is for me to keep ahead of our bills. I don't want to be a nag, but I know he is smoking weed again and maybe even snorting coke. "I don't know for sure about the cocaine, but I smell the marijuana on his clothes." She is crying.

Sighing and heart sick, I gently say. "Listen, Annie. None of this is OK. The fact that he laid hands on you is enough for you to kick him out. You don't know if he is taking good care of your children while you are down here. It seems to me that he is a smoking gun. You are not nor should you even attempt to take responsibility for his actions. You should tell him he has to leave now and that when he gets a job and is settled in his own place for a few months, then maybe the two of you can work things out." I move closer to her put my arms around her. "You can get counseling through some agencies that are available to you. I can help with that; I can put you in touch with a couple of organizations." She lays her head on my shoulder and appears defeated.

"You don't understand, Donna. I love him. I know he can change he has so much pressure on him right now, and I should know better than to nag at him when he is trying his best to help and get some work. He's a good dad and when things are going well, he is a good husband, too. I can't just put him out on the street, I just can't!" she is emphatic.

I squeeze her a little closer. "Annie, you are one of the strongest women I know. How many moms have the courage to pack their children and possessions up and drive thousands of miles on their own to get to safety? You came here with nothing and look what you have done: you have a nice little apartment, you are working at two jobs, you have a great relationship with a very, nice neighbor who takes care of your children at night, and you look after hers in the day. Your children are happy and well-adjusted, and you have created a community around you quickly. Not everyone can do that. You should be proud of what you have accomplished and proud of the mom that you are. Your husband is a grown man. He can look after himself and he is more likely to do this once you stop supporting him and his bad habits. Has he ever hit you before or hurt you in any other way? You have a good friend in Sarah and a haven if things get out of hand."

Sighing she replies. "Yes, that was one of the reasons I packed up and left my family and friends in Prince Albert. I was too ashamed to tell them everything. I know he just needs time to settle and get a job. I know he loves me, Donna. He gave up everything to follow me here. He would not have done that if he didn't love me and our kids. You don't know him; he is so sweet and kind when he is clean and sober and working."

She is getting worked up and defensive. "We've been together for 10 years and it is only in the last few years where he has been under such a lot of stress when he started to drink and do dope. It was after that when things got bad. I know once he is working things will be better. I just can't kick him to the gutter just because things are hard. I'm sorry I ragged on you Donna. Me and the kids will be OK, I just needed to vent. Thanks for listening and caring about us, but we're okay, and I'll be fine. Please don't say anything to Sarah. I don't want my friends and neighbors involved in my business. I can look after myself and my kids. I have to get back to work." Annie stands and walks away in a huff.

"Annie, I'm here at the end of the phone if you need me. Just call. Please look after yourself. I'll see you next week. I love you, Annie, and so does Jesus." Dejected and a little annoyed at myself for jumping in with both feet instead of just listening and supporting Annie. I head to another corner to see another girl.

"I love you too Donna," she calls out.

I chat with Sandy and then go home. I want to talk to Gipp about Annie and get his advice. Gipp often talks with the women when they come to our home and counsels them when they ask. He teaches them about the Bible when they question him about Christianity.

"I'm so glad you're still up." I hug him when I get home.

"Tough night? You look exhausted," he says, hugging me back.

I tell him about Annie and how worried I am that she will get hurt or worse if she continues to allow her husband to stay in her home.

He gently eases me onto the couch and sits next to me. "You can only do what you are doing, just keep listening and support her in every way you can, the decision ultimately is one Annie must make. If things get physical and dangerous, then we can talk more about it with her. You don't want to push and alienate her so that she pushes you away. She will take care of her children; she did it before when she packed them up and moved here. She's stronger than she thinks she is. Be there and we will do all we can to help when she is ready to accept our help. Now, you need to get some sleep." He takes my hand.

I lay my head on his shoulder and sigh. "I know you are right, Gipp. It's just so hard to see her face bruised and the fear and confusion in her eyes. She loves him and believes he loves her. It seems from what Annie tells me that he is a good dad, but I remember that Sarah told me he yells at the kids at night when Annie is at work. I know, I know ... parents yell at their kids all the time. She didn't know what was going on at the time. I know Annie would never let him hurt them, it just gets dicey knowing he may not only be smoking weed but taking stronger drugs as well. I'd like to know where he gets the money to buy that stuff if he is not working." I snip.

"I hear what you are saying Donna." He eases me off the couch. "Again, that is not information you have and really it is not our business until Annie brings us in to help. You really only know what Sarah tells you not only about the situation here, but any information Annie might have told her about Prince Albert. Maybe you should phone Sarah in the morning and put her on alert that things are not that great and ask her to keep an eye on things. She can hear any loud noises or yelling coming from Annie's. Annie can't know you have put Sarah on guard. Do not go into details about what Annie confided in you. It is up to her to tell who she wants. C'mon to bed. I'm tired and I've got an early appointment in the morning. We can't do anymore tonight." We both head to bed.

"Tomorrow's another day," I sigh. "Good night."

"Good night. Sweet dreams," he whispers back.

October 11, 2015

Three weeks have gone by and all seems to be better with Annie, I haven't seen any more signs of abuse and she seems upbeat when I talk with her. She has not said anything more about what is going on at home, so I assume things have settled down. I don't bring up the subject, I simply ask her how things are going and leave it up to her if she wants me to know any more. I feel uneasy about this. Inside I am afraid. She is vulnerable. She has two little children so she can't just up and leave again, at least not easily like she could if she were on her own. I always feel a little afraid when I walk away from her each week, wondering if things are OK and if she has anyone she can talk to. I know the ball is in her park, and I need to be certain that she knows I am here for her.

When I approach Annie tonight, I can see she is not OK. She has dark circles under her eyes, her hair is held back with an elastic, she has little make-up on, and no lipstick. It looks like she grabbed any colour clothes. They certainly don't blend well, colourful but not coordinated like she usually wears.

"Hi Annie, how is it going?" I ask handing her a bag. It is still nice weather even though we are nearing the month of November.

She looks depressed. "Oh, Donna, I don't know what to do anymore. Children's services have been called in because Len phoned them and told them what I do for work at night, "she whispers.

I'm surprised by that. "Why in the world would he do that? Have they contacted you personally or have you only heard it from Len?

"Because he tried to get welfare money to support them. No, they haven't called me yet, that's why I am trying to get him out so they can see how well I look after my kids, without him. I can't reason with him anymore; he is so volatile. I need him to get out, but he says I am an unfit mother because of what I do. I told him we wouldn't eat or be able to pay rent if it wasn't for this job. I can't earn enough money waitressing or cleaning to support my children. He says that's no excuse for me to be whoring myself." She is angry now.

While she continues to vent every detail of their ongoing battles, I think it odd that Annie has not been, at the least, interviewed by Children's Services, if indeed Len lodged a complaint.

"I slapped him, and he shoved me and then punched me in the stomach and kept shoving me. I feel like my ribs are broken, or at least cracked, I can hardly breathe. He's like an animal when he gets mad, and I don't know what to do. I am so afraid of him but if I go to the authorities, I could lose my kids." She is pacing now. "I can't prove any of the things he does or says to me. If children's services, follow up on his accusations I could be in a whole lot of trouble. I wish he were dead; I can't stand him to be around us anymore. He is so volatile, and he hates me!" She is livid.

I try to settle her by sitting down on the steps that are close. Brr, the cement is cold on my bottom.

I pat the place beside me. "C'mon and sit down over here, Annie. Let's try and figure out what we can do. Does anyone else know what is going on? The police are your friends not your enemy, when you call them there is a record of the abuse. Have you been to a doctor for any of your injuries? Even if you have bruises, you need to show your doctor, you need proof he is beating on you. You also need to call the police if he lays a hand on you any time, Annie. This is not normal behavior and there are laws to protect you and your children. Does he go after or yell at the kids? I struggle to remain calm.

She stares at me with disdain and rejects my question with a wave of her hand. "No, no he would never hurt them. It's just me he hates, all because I do this. I know he is doing drugs again; I think that is why he is so mean. He was like this in Prince Albert; that is why I left. I knew no one would believe me because everybody there loved him, and he had so many friends. Even my parents loved him and if I tried to talk to them, they would just tell me to be grateful he was a good husband and father. 'He has a good job and you and your children want for nothing,' they'd say. They just couldn't see he was getting different, and I was his target. He made sure that the excuses for the bruises and black eyes were funny accidents and I became known as being accident prone. I just couldn't stay there any longer. I was more alone there among friends and family than when I arrived here, where I knew on one. I soon found many caring people right away. I don't know what to do, I am so afraid," her anger mutates to sorrow and frustration.

"You need to do what is best for you and your children. It is clear this situation is not working. You are not responsible for your husband's well-being. He is an adult who has and continues to make poor choices. He will drag you down with him, Annie, if you don't resolve this." I sound like a broken record, but I don't know what else to say without putting her on the defensive.

She slumps and tears slip down her cheeks. "I can't just kick him out Donna, I just can't. He is the father of my children and they need him in their life. I believe he is really trying but it is so hard to find a job that suits him and his skills. He is a good man. I know once he gets a job, things will get a lot better, and we may even be able to come together like a real family." She is pleading with me to agree with her.

I feel exasperated. "Annie, I'm watching you riding a rollercoaster. You are slowly being crushed under the stress of what is essentially Len's shortcomings. I can't tell you what to do, but please think about what this might be doing to your children, you are so emotionally starved for affection and support that you likely can't see what is happening to them. You must do what is best for you and them. Len is not your problem and you can't continue to allow him to keep taking advantage of you. I suggest, I hold my hand up, and it is only a suggestion but a strong one: give him an ultimatum. Tell him he has two weeks to find work, any work. So, what if he can't find work that suits him, as you put it. He needs to find work now to help with expenses. Just please look at your alternatives, if things continue as they are, that is all I ask." Now I am pleading!

"I will, Donna, I promise. I have to get back to work but thank you for your help." She slips away emotionally and physically.

December 15, 2015

As the weeks go by, I watch Annie get more and more agitated and depressed. I am certain she is smoking weed and maybe even something stronger and I am increasingly worried about her. She is losing weight and looks lost and alone. She keeps assuring me things are better at home, but from my perspective I don't see that. I see her sadness in the way she holds herself, shoulders are slumped, and her smile never touches her eyes. She pays less and less attention to her clothes and hair.

This is a situation that is stressful for me, too. I keep telling myself I am not qualified to give advice and that I need to simply be a support for her. My constant badgering her is not going to help the situation and what it will do is make her even more defensive and more supportive of Len. I am weak when it comes to Annie. I agonize about her and her children. I promise myself I will back off with suggestions. I can no longer allow myself to do anything other than ask how things are, hoping she will be open and honest. To you the reader you probably wonder why

I don't walk away, but I can't. She is a part of my heart. I wonder if a lot of her feelings might be heightened by a sense of guilt. All I can do is keep a close watch, continue to connect with her children by taking extra food, some clothing like underwear and socks, books for them to read, and other small items to keep a close connection. I seldom see her husband, but I notice evidence of his being there. His clothes laying around on the couch, a jacket on the back of a chair, an ashtray with cigarette butts in it, and other small signs. I wish I could confront him, but I know that would be a major mistake, Annie would simply come to his defense and I might lose any influence I have. I pray each night for her and her little ones. I only wish with all my heart I could do more to lift her spirits. I miss that young woman who had so much hope and determination to make her life here safe and happy. Her joy and enthusiasm of being here, always telling me she loved watching the sunshine come each day, and how that sunshine gave her so much hope and warmed her soul as well as her being.

* * *

This is the most difficult part of this ministry, walking on eggshells trying to keep a balance of helping and not interfering. I know her life is on a downward spiral and I need to keep that connection. I don't want to get a call that she has committed suicide or maybe even murder. I know that sounds a little over the top, but believe me, I have seen both scenarios played out in the early days of this ministry. I experienced days of depression after one suicide. My heart ached like an open wound and I carried such guilt and sorrow that led me to believe I had failed. I know this is not true, but I love these women with such a depth of feeling, I just can't handle all the sorrows that death leaves in its wake.

Enough, I tell myself. It serves no purpose for me to imagine this situation going sideways.

January 21, 2016

It is a cold but sunny day. I am out walking my little dog, Pippa, when my cellphone rings. I glance at the screen and see that it is Annie calling.

"Hi, Annie. What's up?"

No hello just words running together. "Can you come over, right now! Please! Len is here and he has agreed to talk with you and me together to work out how we can be together in a way that works for us both. I really need for you to do this Donna. Please come now," she pleads.

"I'm walking my dog right now, Annie. I am at least a half an hour away from my house. I'll come over in about an hour. Can you and Len wait that long?" I hear Annie talking to Len.

I listen to her muffled words to Len. "Can you wait for about an hour till she gets here, Lenny, she's walking her dog. It'll take that long for her to get home and over here." He says yes Donna, thank you so much for doing this. We'll see you soon." The phone goes dead.

I finish my walk, clean up, and drive over to Annie's apartment. I ring the buzzer so she can let me in the building.

"Hi, Annie, Len, and you two little sweeties. How are you?"

The children run to me and give my knees a big hug. I kneel and gather the two of them in a hug. I am happy to see they are looking well and seem incredibly happy.

"OK, both of you, we're going over to Auntie Sarah's. You and she are going to bake some cookies while mommy and daddy talk with Donna. She looks at Len, I'll be right back. Len, please pour her some coffee," she says as she walks out the door and across the hall.

Annie is back in a few minutes.

"OK, what's going on?" I ask.

She is animated and excited. "Lenny and I just want your help to work out a way for us to be together that is okay for us both."

"I'm guessing all of the changes that have taken place since you arrived in Victoria Len may be causing a rift between you two. Things aren't working for you now, so what's changed where you need me to sort this out for you? You must know Annie and I have tried to work out a solution several times since you moved in here."

Len seems like your average guy and in watching he and Annie interact here, I wonder at the violent friction that so often builds between them so quickly. Over the time he has been here Annie has admitted to me she hates him. I am hesitant to step in here because of their volatile reaction to one another when they don't get their way.

He looks like any other guy and has a quiet demeanor about him. That is probably because I am here. He has carrot-red hair and a goatee. Blue eyes that bore right into mine: he does look right into my eyes when he is speaking to me. It is a bit unsettling. He is about six feet or better and neatly dressed in a shirt, top button open at the neck, blue jeans and boots. His black leather jacket is neatly hanging off the back of his chair. He just seems like an average guy. I know better, though, looks can be deceiving. I cannot sit in judgment, but I carry a deep anger toward any man who lays hands on a woman.

I feel uncomfortable. I don't know Len that well and I don't think I am the best person to do this, but it is a step forward for Annie to ask in front of Len.

Len takes the lead, standing and with authority, says. "We need an outside opinion on how we can work through this mess, obviously, Annie doesn't believe I am doing the best I can do to get a job that pays a decent salary so I can help with the expenses. I am here helping to take care of the kids when she is at work." The more he talks the more worked up he is getting.

"I can't be here all day and look for work at the same time. She expects me to help around here and nags at me every time I don't jump when she tells me to do something." He is pacing now.

"She wants me to take a dead-end job that pays minimum wage just so she can trap me into doing every little thing she deems urgent. Well, I'm not her trained puppy who's willing to jump every time she says how high. I know I can get the work I am good at and that pays me a good salary. I don't need her to hound me every minute I am here." Lenny continues to pace back and forth during his tirade.

"That's not fair Lenny," Annie whines. "You don't do anything to help in the day when you are here, you don't go looking for a job every day like you should. I believe you're snorting coke and smoking weed. Some days you're so doped up, I can't even talk to you. How are you going to work when you're high? Even if you took a low-paying job while you are looking for a better one, you could help me and the kids." She is looking more downtrodden.

He lashes out and Annie squirms. "I help you now. I feed the kids supper, put them to bed while you're out doing what you do all night long! If you had a decent job, it wouldn't be like this. How do you think I feel, knowing what you're doing every night while I sit here and imagine all sorts of things? You should have thought of that when you knew I would come after you. You had no right to take my kids away from me! Len yells and moves toward her angrily.

Annie gets up and steps away putting her arms in front as if she is protecting herself. "You left me no choice, you were drinking, and smoking weed every night. I was afraid of you. You know our families always supported you because you supported me and the kids and 'we wanted for nothing.' They always thought you were the best dad and husband. They didn't know about the booze and drugs. They were never going to admit you were the problem," she is yelling now.

This is getting out of hand. I am scared that Len is going to get more violent and Annie is getting more aggressive. I step up and take Annie's arm and gently ask her sit back down. I turn to Len and ask him to please take a seat before this escalates further.

"OK, OK, enough," I say. "Both of you please settle down if you want my help then I beg you to listen to what I have to say. None of what is being said here is helping anyone; you both might as well pour gasoline on the fire you are stoking. Len, if you lay a hand on Annie, I will call the police. Annie, yelling is getting you nowhere. Both of you need to think about what you want from each other. What will work, not just for you two but for your children as well. Len, do you think it is fair to expect Annie to pay all the expenses and carry the emotional load of trying to keep this a good home for your children? What about your drinking and doing drugs? Do you really believe that is OK?" I ask, tentatively. I am unnerved and I know I am in over my head. I also know I need to do what I can to defuse this.

Sneering he responds. "I'm not an addict; I am just so stressed by her always nagging at me. That is my real reason for drinking. If she would just give me some breathing room while I try and sort things out, things would be good. She exaggerates a lot; there was more than just my drinking that caused her to leave. Her parents knew she was hooking some back home, too, and she smoked as much as I did. She never has considered my feelings when it comes to her prostituting herself; she told me it was just for the money. I was making good money there. She was into weed as much as I was, maybe more." He is calmer but on the defensive.

Annie jumps right in. "What do you mean, things would be good? You are doing exactly what you did in Prince Albert. Why did you follow me here? Why didn't you stay in Prince Albert with your no-good friends? You scared me, you shoved me around and I was sure you were going to beat me up or hurt our kids. You were totally out of control. You were no help to me or your children, and you nearly lost a damn good job. Now you're here doing the same rotten stuff and expecting me to put up with it. Well, no more! You can pack your things a get out!" Annie spews losing control.

I am seeing a side of Annie I have never seen before. She is quick to anger and very confrontational. Len is so busy feeling sorry for himself he ends up blaming Annie for his own short fuse and bad behavior.

"You think I'm going to leave my kids here with while you're out whoring all over this city?" He looks bewildered.

I am exasperated and once again, I interrupt their fighting, with trepidation I snap. "That's enough, both of you. Settle down and let's see how we can work this out. You're both too emotional to think straight right now. I am going to offer some suggestions, if you don't take them for now, I am going to leave. Len you will need to leave with me. If you refuse, I will call the police from my car. Len would you consider getting a job not in your field, something that would bring in some money to help Annie with expenses? Annie, do you want Len to stay here or not? This is your apartment and if you want him to find his own place to live than you need to give him time to do that. Maybe a week to find a job and a place to live until you can both decide what you want on a permanent basis."

I feel out of my depth and want this to end so I can get out of here. I wish I had had the smarts to tell them I don't have the training to do this and suggest they look for an experienced counsellor but no, here I am again in over my head!

Annie jumps up. "I don't want you to leave Lenny, but I need you to help me out here. You could get another job at that little restaurant where you worked for the first couple of weeks when you first got here. You could still put your name in other places where you would rather work. The kids are so happy you are here, but I can't let you bring your drinking here." Annie adds, totally surrendering.

And there is one of the problems. Annie is quick to acquiesce.

Now Len is pleading. "Don't ask me to go back to that no-win job. I know I can get a better job; I promise I'll go out every day and look for something I like. You need to just back off and let me do this. I'll stop drinking and doing drugs, I promise. Just give me a couple of weeks to do better. But please, don't yell at me in front of our kids. I know they don't understand. Sometimes when you do that, it makes me feel impotent that's when I get angry. I get angry and embarrassed. My kids don't need to hear that crap you spew." His pain and outrage are palpable. "I love my kids and I need to be with them. Let's try and work things out over the next couple of weeks. Please Annie, I got nowhere to go, and I don't know anyone here who can help me. I just want what's best for my kids. I promise I'll help more. Just give me a couple of weeks to work things out." Now he is asking Annie rather than making demands.

She succumbs. "OK Lenny let's do this together. I want you here with me and the kids. I just can't have you drinking or doing drugs. You need to find a job and straighten your life out. I'll give you two weeks to find a job and no drugs or booze or you're out of here. I'm serious." She is smiling and moves toward him as if she is going to hug him. Len steps back.

I am relieved they have come to a tentative agreement. I am not convinced any of this will work for long. I want out of here and next time I promise myself I will not get in the middle of this kind of situation ever again. I take a seat and look at them both.

"All right, I hope you can do this," I say. "Annie I'll see you later in the week and, Len, please do this for your kids as well as for yourself. I can't tell either one of you what to do, but I believe if things don't change over the next two weeks, then there is no alternative: Len, you will have to leave." I hug Annie, shake Len's hand, and leave.

January 28, 2016

It has only been a week since I last saw Annie and Len. I walk up to Annie on her corner and notice the dark shadows under her unfocused eyes. Alarm bells go off in my brain and I take a second look at her. She looks a little disheveled. Annie is usually well groomed, and her outfits are always nicely coordinated. She almost always has a bright smile and carefree attitude when she is working. Tonight, I am certain she is on something illegal. She just looks off. She has on a pair of jeans and a heavy black sweater under her parka which is open. All dark colours, no jewelry, little makeup, and a cap that is also dark and not very flattering, with her hair all tucked under it.

"Hi Annie, how is everything in your world?" I am trying to be casual, so I don't turn her away from me. I hand her one of my gift bags and gently hold her hand a little longer than usual.

"I'm good, Donna. I'm having a busy night so don't have too long to jag with you." She takes the bag and walks away.

"Hey Annie, wait a minute. What's up with you tonight? You look beat! Talk to me, just take a few minutes and tell me what's going on." I catch up with Annie and walk alongside her.

She wheels around facing me. "You want to' know what's up? I'll tell you. After your long lecture to Lenny and me, we had a big blowout. He is behaving like he owns me. I can hardly keep up with his demands and expenses, not only regular ones but ones he is racking up with his drug dealer. I can't trust him with my kids anymore, so I must pay Sarah to look after them at night until I get home. Sometimes Len gets there before me and forces Sarah to go back to her own apartment and I quote! 'leave him to hell alone.' Those were his exact words. He's lucky that Jim didn't come over." Seething, she continues her outburst.

"So no, I am not the greatest tonight or any night. I know I should never had let him move in, but that's water under the bridge now. I feel trapped. I don't know how to get him out without involving the cops or children's services. I could take my kids and go to a woman's shelter, but that won't work because I must come out sometime. My kids love their dad; they just see the good side of him. He's great with them he plays, reads to them, takes them on hikes, and they adore him. How can I stop that? I'm always the bad guy in their eyes, I do all the disciplining and make them do small chores." She continues her diatribe becoming more animated, stomping back and forth.

"Then he comes in and undermines my authority and we end up screaming and yelling at each other and the kids are caught in the middle. Sometimes, I notice the look on their faces, and I shrink in horror at what we are doing to them. I feel trapped. I ran away from him and what does he do? He follows me here and brings his crappy attitude and bad habits with him. The first opportunity he takes to play on my sympathy, what do I do? I fold and let it all happen again. I am such a creep, so weak, so needy, such a loser!" She sits on the building steps and puts her head in her hand in defeat.

I see fear, surrender and gut-wrenching grief, knowing she feels that she has no good way out.

"Oh Annie." I enfold her in my arms and just let her seethe.

I take a deep breath and try once again to get her to take some positive action. "You can do this, you're not alone. I will do everything in my power to help you. There are ways out of this. We can look at your options together. Let me get my lawyer friend, Will, to let Len know you will take legal action if he doesn't leave now. You've already given him two weeks-notice to get out if he is not willing to abide by your rules. He has made it clear he doesn't care a wit about your feelings."

Annie squirms and tells me. "It's only when I get on his case. I think he gets scared when I get in his face. He wouldn't have left his friends, his job and his family if he didn't love me Donna. You don't see him doing good stuff for me, you just see the bad stuff." Now she is getting miffed at me!

You can't change him Annie. He is out of control and you need to rein him in and get him out and away from your children. I hear myself and know I sound like a broken record. I simply do not know how much more I can do to convince her to act.

I sigh and speak quietly. "You need to get some normalcy back in your lives. We can do this, Annie; you are not alone, you have friends here, you have Sarah, the women you work with, Gipp and myself and Reenie even though she is in Prince Albert, you both have a phone. You just need to be strong and be willing to stand up to him. You can take a standing order out, allowing him limited access to you and the children. You can ensure that his visits will have to be outside of the apartment. Please let me call Will. I know he will help, and it won't cost you anything I promise." I speak quietly, silently praying she will agree to meet with Will.

She snorts. "It's no good, Donna. He has already called children's services once and they believe everything he tells them. He will tell him about what I do and make it sound like I leave the kids alone at night and that I bring my dates into my home. I know him; you don't. I can't push him, or he'll make sure he gets to take my kids. I can't let that happen. He will lie and say whatever he needs to, just to make my life a living hell. It was like this in Prince Albert. My family and friends all were on his side." She bristles, turning her anger back at Len.

Alarm bells go off in my head. Why would her family and her best friend be on Len's side if his behavior was like this? I only have Annie's side of the stories and that Len is the husband she ran from. But that is a conversation for another time.

I am now hesitant as I prattle on. "Annie, you have a neighbor in Sarah who can vouch for how well you have cared for your children. I will tell them how you stepped up and left his abusive behavior and drove all the way here to protect them and get away from him. I can vouch for how you found a lovely little apartment, furnished it, and made it a warm and happy place for you and your kids. You have so much more going for you than he has."

I take a deep breath she looks forlorn and lost. "You need to fight, Annie; you can't let him keep the upper hand. One of these nights, everything will get so out of control that one of you will do something you will live to regret and could involve criminal charges that results in loss of your children. Please let me call Will and at least talk to him about this." I turn to her and look right into her eyes while I am speaking.

She turns away and stands. "OK, OK, you go ahead, but you can't bring him around when Lenny is there. I want to talk to Will and find out exactly how we can do this, so no one gets hurt and I get to keep my kids and my place. He needs to get out and we can plan for him to come and take the children out and do stuff with them, but he can never come to get them at my place. I will meet him and give them over to him and I will come back and pick them up once their allotted time is over." She is already dictating her terms.

She wipes her face, and I can see the Annie I first met, but I know those shadows under her eyes won't go away until she gets Len out of her life. He will continue to make her life a living hell and haunt her dreams. Who knows what he is on and just how volatile he can get? My stomach is churned up. I give her a hug, say goodnight, tell her to call me anytime, and I go home. I feel defeated and uneasy at the same time. I wonder if I am wrong about some of what I believe. I believe Annie would not lie, but she might not remember the details clearly. I am in a conundrum. I make a decision to go forward and contact Will and see how that turns out.

February 18, 2016

It takes two weeks to set up a time with Will. The next problem is trying to sync those times with Annie when Len is not at the apartment. Finally, three weeks pass, and we coordinate our times. Will and I arrived at Annie's around 1 p.m. I whisper my feelings and thoughts to Will before he knocks on the door.

"I know Annie will be extremely nervous and anxious about this meeting with Will. She is torn between her love for her husband and the knowledge that he is a powder keg waiting to explode. She waffles between accusing him of outlandish behavior, which includes physical abuse as well as emotional trauma. She applauds his love of his children and that she knows he is trying to be a good husband and provider. She should know it is only a matter of time before this situation becomes extremely dangerous for herself and her children." I nervously tell him my fears.

He looks a little annoyed. "Relax, Donna. I have some experience in situations such as this and I have diffused them successfully many times. I know what to expect. I need you to keep your thoughts to yourself. I don't mean to upset you, but you need to understand this is Annie's battle and not yours. Your remarks will be tainted by your feelings and beliefs and not hers. You need to trust that I understand what is going on. You should also remember you are only getting Annie's side of the story. I need to approach this situation with an unbiased opinion. Now let's do this." He lays his hand on my back and moves us forward to knock on Annie's door.

"Hi, Annie," I say as she answers the door. "This is my friend Will, the lawyer I told you about.,"

"Hi, Donna. Of course, please come in. I have coffee ready and some cookies the kids and I made for you. I hope you like them; the kids are extremely excited to know what you think. They added some special ingredients, just for you."

"Wow, that sounds exciting and scary at the same time. I ask the children. "Will you tell me what you added, or is that a secret? "Yes!" they both squeal bouncing up and down on their little legs. They look good and crunchy. I absolutely would like a cup of coffee and maybe if it's OK, two cookies. How about you, Will?" I smile at him.

"Uh, sure that sounds like a good idea. Maybe just one cookie for me. I try to limit sweets between meals, but I'd love one and a cup of coffee," he smiles back.

"Okay, guys," Annie says to the kids, "let's serve them cookies and coffee and then you can take some over to Sarah and Jamie. We won't be that long and after we'll all go to Beacon Hill park and have one of those delicious ice cream cones. The goats should be out on such a nice sunny day.," Annie packs up some cookies and takes her children over to Sarah.

She looks nervous as she comes back into the apartment.

"Annie, I know this is exceedingly difficult for you," says Will. "It is even harder in that you don't know me, but I am here to listen, and I hope that I can offer you some solutions that will work for you and still be comfortable for you. I am not here to judge you or your husband. I am here to listen to what you want to tell me." Will takes her hand and gently leads her to a comfortable chair and sits across from her. I sit on a chair near the table.

She is nervously wringing her hands and seems to be avoiding eye contact with Will. "This is really hard for me. I want you to know that I love Lenny. I just can't have him stay here while he is so uptight. He is taking drugs and drinking. He loses his temper with me and I am scared for my kids and myself. If anything happens to me, he will get custody of them, and I can't stand by and let that happen. Things have been good the last couple of weeks. He seems to be a lot better since Donna and I talked with him. I know he is trying, if only he would leave the drugs and booze alone, we would be okay." she barely takes breath.

She shifts a little and runs her hands through her hair. "I understand why he is caving: he can't find the job he wants, and I know he feels guilty that he can't help me with expenses. I'm not defending him, but I need you to understand the stress and pressure he is under. I am afraid he might do something drastic if we keep going the way we are. I just need him to find his own place while we work out a better solution for all of us. If he does that, I promise

I will let him have the children for playtime in the parks and playgrounds. I don't want him coming here to pick them up or drop them off. I don't want him taking them to his place either. I know he will have illegal stuff there and once he starts drinking, he gets out of control." Annie is so anxious she is almost babbling, trying to tell Will what she wants from Len.

"I understand what you are saying, Annie," Will gently responds, but you must understand that once we get a standing order, in place, you and he cannot have any contact whatsoever."

"No, no I don't want the police dragged into this. Lenny is not a criminal, Will; he is just so stressed right now. This isn't who he really is. We need to be gentle with him and persuade him to get his own place while we work things out." She is whining and tears are leaking.

It is hard for me to sit and not say anything. Annie is upset and starting to once again defend Len's behavior.

He takes Annie's hand and asks if she would like a glass of water, which she declines. "I hear you, Annie, but from what Donna has told me Len is pretty well out of control now. You need to think about your own safety and that of your children. You pointed out yourself that if anything happens to you, he will likely get custody of your children or, worse, end up in jail and there will be no one there for your children. I know that is not what you want, either.

He pauses and takes a sip of coffee. "I am hearing just your side of this Annie; I can't sit in judgement of Len. I am trying to make a recommendation based on what you are telling me. You have a difficult decision to make here,

I don't want to influence you either way. I am asking you to think seriously about what you want to do. You cannot have it both ways. Either you get him removed from this apartment and temporarily out of your life while he gets his act together—that means he gets a job, a place of his own, and off the drugs and liquor—or you let things stay as they are and continue to fight off his verbal and physical attacks. Remember, your children are witness to this behavior and that is very damaging to them. It must be very upsetting for them to watch you fighting each other. You can't control what he does nor can he control you, but you can take some positive steps to eliminate the chance of him hurting you or them." Will says gently but firmly.

She starts to waffle again, defending Len. "I know he would never hurt his children, but I can't take them away from him again," Annie pleads. "There must be some other way we can bring Lenny around. Maybe if you talked to him and tell him that if he doesn't stop drugs and drinking, then we will take out this standing order. I know if he stops taking all that rotten stuff, he will be a different person. He used to be such a caring and loving man before he started drinking."

"I'm sorry you had to watch that decline, Annie," Will counters. "You have to make a difficult decision here. I believe a Standing Order, is a good option and the one I support. I believe it might antagonize your husband if I meet with him and threaten him. I can only make suggestions that I think work best for you and your children. I am willing to do what is legally necessary to put it in place at no charge to you. You can let me know if you decide to go forth with this. I am concerned for you and your children. I have seen domestic problems end in disaster. The outcome is seldom good for the children. I'll leave you my card and I'll wait to hear from you Annie."

He stands up and shakes her hand, gently placing his hand on her back.

"I thank you for the delicious cookie and the coffee. Now, I must be on my way. I have another appointment in an hour. Take good care of yourself and your children, Annie. They were very well-behaved, and I can see how much you love and care for them. Please remember that when you consider what you might have to do to diffuse this situation.

He turns and shakes my hand, saying. "Don't be a stranger, come out and join Heather and me for dinner sometime."

After he leaves Annie turns on me and berates me. "Oh Donna, you didn't tell me it would be like this, I thought he would come up with a solution that would help Lenny and me, not threaten Lenny. How can he ask me to involve the police? That will put Len over the top. He will be so distraught that I would do such a terrible thing to him, he might kill himself. I can't do that; I just can't, nor do I want to take any standing order against him!" Annie sits at the table next to me, whimpering and cradling her head in her hands.

I stand up, trying not to be offended by her blaming me for Will's suggestions. "Annie, you are not doing anything terrible to Len, you are simply putting a legal document in place to ensure he can't come near you or your children until he cleans up. He is bringing this on himself. This is just a temporary solution that will give you both time to settle your volatile emotions and take a breather. It will be the best thing for you and the kids, I promise. It will keep you safe. When things calm down and he is more settled, you can both come to a workable solution.

I feel deflated and worn out listening to her insisting that none of this is Len's fault. I am realizing I am flogging a dead horse and Annie is not going to change her thinking.

I wearily continue. "This decision is yours to make. We have given you all the information and tools to protect yourself and your children. You cannot control your husband. I need to get on home, Annie; you can let me know or you can call Will yourself and set this thing in motion. Try not to wait too long to decide. Thank you, Annie for meeting with Will. I'll see you downtown on Thursday night, or you can call me anytime if you need anything or if you just want to talk."

February 25, 2016

It has been a tense couple of days since I left Annie. I have not heard from her. I don't know if Will has heard anything and I don't want to put my nose where it does not belong. He would honor client privilege I am sure and, besides, I don't want to put that between us.

My phone rings, jarring me out of my thoughts.

"Hello?"

"Hi Donna, it's Cherie. Man! I just got away from a ridiculous and humiliating situation. You'll never guess what happened to me. I'm so mad, I am spitting bullets!"

"What in the world happened, Cherie?" Cherie is really animated when she describes situations with me. She is vibrant, pretty and chic. Her hair is a mass of black curls that bounce all over when she is speaking. Her skin is a gorgeous coffee with cream colour enhanced by her almond-coloured eyes. Her hands are always in motion. Even on the phone I can hear her voice quivering.

"I'll tell you what happened. I was on a call and we were getting on with everything when his wife came home early. Fortunately for him, she called out to him when she came in the house. He picked me up, grabbed my clothes and boots, and shoved me out the bedroom window. I am startled to find myself sitting on the grass with not a stitch on and the neighbor looking out her window. She watched as I put my clothes on with as much dignity as I could muster up. I gently pulled on my boots, struggled to get my coat on, stood up and with a charming smile, I waved goodbye to her. Honestly, if you could have seen the expression on her face, you would laugh yourself silly. What a jerk that guy was. Fortunately, I got my money up front. I can't believe he did that to me," she sputters.

"Well, I guess he was pretty freaked out to be in that situation." I start to chuckle. I can't help it; it sounds so bazaar and as I visualize the whole scene, I start to laugh.

"What's so funny?"

"I'm sorry, Cherie, but you must admit it sounds crazy and funny!" I am laughing uncontrollably.

"Some friend you are," she sputters and then starts to laugh, too. We are giggling, I'm holding my side the whole thing is so hilarious.

We finally settle down and I offer to meet her for a cup of coffee.

"I can't. I have an appointment in an hour, and I have a couple of errands I need to get done now. I'm glad I called, thanks for caring, we'll do this again sometime when I need your sympathy!" She is laughing as she hangs up the phone.

I laugh myself silly and finally get a grip. Whenever I get that picture in my head, I laugh and laugh. It really is hilarious.

I need to get my little bags ready for tonight and it is already 5 p.m.

* * *

I visit with Tammy and Misty and spot Annie on her corner.

"Hi, Annie. How's it going?"

"Hi, Donna. It's good; I'm busy tonight. Things are great at home. Lenny is being a big help and he seems to be off his drugs. He's looking after the kids at night again and he's always in bed when I get home. I think our talks are really helping a lot," she says, keeping her face turned from me.

"What's that on your face, Annie? It looks like a cut or something," I ask and walk around her to see a massive black eye. I also notice her holding her stomach, wincing as she tries to turn away from me.

I fire questions at her not giving her a chance to respond, I am so upset and scared. "Did Lenny do this? Is this his way of coming around and being great? Why do you insist on trying to protect him Annie? This is so bad, please do something or get the police involved to stop it Annie!"

I am angry with her and with Lenny and all I can do is wonder if their children are at home alone with this guy or not. They could even be left alone while he goes out and does whatever the heck he does when Annie is not there. I don't know if Sarah is still looking after them.

She shouts at me telling me again. "It was my fault, Donna. I kept nagging him. He told me to shut up, he was really, mad. I should have stopped, but I just wanted him to help me with the laundry because he was just laying around and not doing anything. I know I shouldn't have threatened him when I told him I had a lawyer and I was going to get a stopping order or something, to get him out until he got his life together and that I needed to be left alone so I could work my own problems out. She took a breath and went on, calmly now.

"I told him I could no longer pay all the bills while he did nothing but eat us out of house and home. I called him a lazy bum. I shouldn't have done that. He was furious and he hit me in the face and pushed me down. I hit my side hard. I feel like I have a broken rib or something."

I feel sorry for her, she looks so miserable. "Awe, Annie, when are you going to get your own life together? You have all the information in front of you all you need do is pick up the phone and call Will and it's done. What is holding you back? You can't keep making excuses for Len, you need to act and put a stop to it." I am pleading with her, embracing her. I feel her wince when I hold her.

I am shaking, fearful for her. "No one else can do this Annie—it's on you. Your children are at risk. You can stand there and tell me he would never hurt them, but if he's drugged out or drunk you don't know what he will do. Look at you, you're a battered mess. How much more can you take Annie? Your children aren't deaf and blind—they can see and hear what is happening. They must be terrified when they see you like this." I am frustrated and scared as hell for her and the kids.

"They weren't home when this happened. They were having a playdate at the park with Sarah and Jamie," she spewed at me. She was incredibly angry with me now as well.

Annie, for goodness-sake I beg you to ask yourself—do you really believe they are not being affected by what you two are doing? Even if that weren't so, what right do you have to put yourself in jeopardy? Who do you think will be their caregiver if he beats you up so badly you have to go to the hospital?"

She challenges me looking defiant. "You don't know how hard it is for me! You have everything you need. You think I don't care about my kids, well I do, and I know their father would never hurt them and I need to control my temper and give him a chance. He is stressed; he can't find a job. It's not like he's not looking; he goes out every day and tries. You don't know what he is really like, you have never seen him with his kids, how loving he is and how they adore him, and you don't know what he is like when he is off his drugs. You don't have any right to judge me. It is none of your business how I live my life." She shoves me away.

I am holding on to my own anger and try to convince her once again. "You're right, Annie, none of this is any of my business, but you brought me into it. You're right that I only know what you have told me. And if all that has been true, how can you believe he will stop brutalizing you and doping and boozing his life away. He will drag you down with him and Lord only knows what will happen to your kids. They are who I care about right now. I know you're on something and you have been getting into to it more and more. No one, Annie, no one can make you or Len do what you don't want. But trust me when I say, I will make certain that your children are okay. I am still here and will always be here for you, but I can't make you do what is right for you and them. I will see you next week. Try and stay alive until then. I want to give you a hug Annie—will you let me?"

"Of course, Donna, I promise I'm okay." She hugs me back.

I walk away, scared for her and angry with her. I know she is hurting but I need to try and chip away at her notion that she is to blame for him beating on her. Her stress level is way over the top. I say a silent prayer for her safety and her children's well-being.

May 14, 2016

It's as if the die is cast. Annie is on a one-way trip to disaster. I watch her demeanor change over the weeks. She is getting deeper into the drug lifestyle. Every now and then, she shows up with a black eye, split lip, or a limp and holding her sides. I continue to try and talk to her, but she no longer hears what I say. She continues to defend Len's actions, citing his lack of being able to get a job. I am really tempted to call in children's services but know beyond a doubt that her children will be removed from both she and Len. I keep in touch with Sarah, who says she has not seen Annie under the influence of drugs or alcohol. She is concerned that Len continues to mooch off Annie and she does nothing about it. Sarah assures me that Len is kind to his children and cares for them when Annie works at night. She notices his drinking but is oblivious to his drug use. She supports Annie and always tells me the children are well taken care of. I am at my wits end, wondering if Len will one day go too far and one or both she and Len will end up dead or in jail.

Tonight, Annie is very pale and, once again, has bruises on her face. I can see where she has tried to cover them with make-up. She looks nice tonight, though. She has on black leggings with a pretty pink knee-length sweater. She has her little tam on her head, with her curls hugging her face.

I cheerfully greet her, trying not to be confrontational. "Hi Annie, you look lovely tonight, although you are a little pale. Do you feel OK? What's going on? Did you have a bad date?" I ask, although I am certain Len has once again knocked her around.

"Oh no, I tripped over my shoes and fell onto the foot-stool. Boy, did it ever hurt, it feels like a cracked rib to me. I bashed my face on the floor as I knocked the stool side-ways. I'm such a klutz," she chuckles.

I hand her one of my gift bags.

She smiles at me, and laughingly says. "Awe Donna, just what I need, some cologne to spray over my hair. I just washed it and I didn't have any cream rinse so this will do nicely and make me smell sweet at the same time. Oh, and some licorice—I love it and it will give me some energy, I do feel a little tired tonight. I'm OK now, though, thanks to you. These give me a lovely pick-me-up. Thanks so much. I need to get back to work, I haven't been that busy tonight, so if you don't mind moving on to Misty down the street, I will do my thing and hope I make some more money to-night." She is babbling.

I struggle not to say more about how hurt she seems. "OK, Annie, but please remember that I am at the end of a phone whenever you are ready to talk again. I'd love to come over for coffee one afternoon and have a visit with the children. Maybe we can invite Sarah, too. I am happy to bring some pastries, donuts, muffins, cookies, or whatever you would like. I am free Tuesday and Thursday afternoons next week if either of those days work for you." I put my hand on her shoulder and give it a gentle squeeze.

Her smile seems forced. "That's sweet of you, Donna. I will check and see what day works best for me. I know Lenny is going to be out a couple of afternoons looking for work. After the last time, I think it would be best if he weren't home. I'll check with Sarah and see if we can make it work. I will call you Sunday afternoon and let you know. You have a good week." She sashays to her corner.

"Wow!" I say to myself. That was a cold shoulder if ever I saw one. I sure hope I haven't ruined my relationship with Annie. She may not know it, but I am the best friend she will ever have. I love her to pieces and will continue to watch out for her. I am worried, too, about how high she is tonight.

* * *

I find myself in a turmoil over the number of times I have tried to have a conversation with Annie about the seriousness of her situation with Len. It seems that I say the same things to her every time she is beaten up and ends up calling or telling me about it. She makes the same arguments over and over about how it is her fault and if she hadn't done this or that to make him mad, none of it would have happened. This is the same rhetoric we get in most of the cases of partner violence situations where I try to help as best as I can. I am sure most police officers and health care workers called to domestic problems probably hear the same story, too. Trying to get the abused to accuse the abuser of being a bully is like pulling teeth. I believe that, in Annie's case, she is more frightened of losing Len than she is of his bullying. She can't see the forest for the trees, which is why she constantly makes excuses for him. It is like a huge barrier blocking all common sense. Nothing can breach the resulting chasm. I feel as if I am harping on the same problems over and over and I know I sound like a broken record. I need to back off tonight and concentrate on the other women I want to talk with to see how their lives are going.

I walk over to Misty's corner.

"Hi, Misty. You look very pretty, tonight. How's your world?" I hand her one of my gift bags.

"I'm doing really good, Donna. Thanks for the goody bag I love getting this! You're going to be so proud of me when I tell you my news." She twirls around, her multicoloured skirt swirls around her legs. She laughs, cheerfully.

"Well, it must be some great news to make you feel that way."

"It is, it is! I am so excited, Donna. You know how I have been upgrading my grades to get into the nursing program at Camosun College. Well, now I only need to upgrade my English and then I have enough credits to stay on the wait list. In fact, I put my name on the list a while ago. I am registered for the English course and I will be finished that in November. Oh, Donna, I have wanted this for so long and now I am so close to getting it I am scared something will happen and I will screw it up. I have been clean and sober now for six months and I am scared that something bad will happen to me or my husband, Mick, and I will lose the chance when it comes up. Mick stuck with me and married me, how blessed I feel. I wish I could just start the program as soon as I get my passing grade in English; it would be so much easier for me. That two-year wait is murder for someone like me. I get bored or convince myself I'm not good enough or smart enough to do it." She laments.

I take her hand. "Listen to yourself, Misty. Goodness, look at what you have done and how far you have come in the last year. I am enormously proud of you. You can do this. You can easily keep yourself busy for a couple of years. You need to get a different job for one thing. You should look at getting a job as a waitress or maybe in a care home, helping to read to the residents or do basic care for them. You don't want anyone asking you questions about this job; it is best if you start to walk away now. You can always call me and talk to me if you feel yourself wavering. You know you can come and see Gipp and get some counseling on how best to move forward. We will always be in your corner Misty, no matter where or when or what the problem is; all you need to do is call me. You carry one of my pass-it-on cards with you all the time. I know this to be a fact. After you were arrested in Vancouver a couple of years ago, the gal in the cell with you was so impressed when you gave your card to her that she stayed out of the trade and never looked back. Remember what the message was on that card?" I hug her.

She whispers in my ear. "Oh yes, of course I do. It was a picture of a little boy in overalls standing on the sidewalk and the message said, 'Don't worry about tomorrow, God is already there. And I told her that you said we are never alone, that Jesus is always beside us. All we need to do is whisper His name and we will feel His love and peace will surround us.' Remember, too, Donna, that was when I started to go to Camosun to upgrade my high school marks so I could do something to help women like us. Here I am on the brink of fulfilling that dream. I know I can do this; I know I can! Yikes, here comes my date. I need to go. Thanks for tonight, Donna. I will see you next week. I love you!" she says and dashes away.

"I love you back, Misty. Stay safe!"

* * *

What a super bit of news that was. Who would have thought Misty would be where she is today, I am impressed. Two years ago, she was deep into drugs and alcohol and most of the time was either stoned or drunk. Her appearance was terrible, her hair was a mess, and she was skin and bones. She was erratic and unreliable. What a transformation. She is fun to talk to and always has a smile on her face. I believe Micky has a lot to do with her changes. He has been there for her for the last four years. He stuck by her through all her troubles and was a steady influence. I hope I get a chance to tell him that. I can't believe all going well she will be a registered nurse in a few short years. I know she will use her job to help others like her, whether in a hospital or through some organization that reaches out to women and men doing sex work. I pray I am here to see it happen. It is uncanny how most of most of these women's career goals focus on helping others. On that note, I head home, lighthearted, proud, and incredibly happy for Misty.

August 18, 2016

The weeks drift by and each Thursday when I try to talk with Annie, our conversations become more scattered and stinted. I can see the gradual downward spiral she is on. I don't know what her drug of choice is, but I assume it is crystal meth, as it is one of the cheapest drugs to buy on the streets. It quickly rots teeth and ages these young women in a very few years. It is just a guess on my part. It could be any one of many drugs out there that are readily available provided you have the money to pay. About four months pass before I can no longer avoid addressing her addiction head-on. I am tired of dancing around the subject, and I carry such guilt because I know what the score is. I can't stand by and watch her destroy all that she worked for when she first arrived here. This Thursday she is looking totally wasted. Her demeanor and physical appearance are beyond describing.

"Hi Annie, you're not looking so good tonight. What's happening?" I ask as I hand her one of my gift bags.

"Whaddya mean?" she slurs.

"Well, I just need to look at you to know something is not right and the way you slur your words tells me something is really off with you. I know that you know what I am talking about. I also know you probably believe it is none of business what you do. But hear this Annie, I love you and I love your children. What you are doing to yourself and them is a disaster waiting to happen. You should know by now! I won't stand by and watch you throw your life away like this. It is only a matter of time before you tank, and Lord only knows where and when that will happen. Let me help you, please!" I hope my desperation doesn't show, but I am deeply concerned.

She struggles to stand straight and tall. "Ya knowwat Donna, what I do with my life is none of your business. And for your information, I am in complete control of it. I don't need you to tell me what I can and can't do, so back off. I'm tired of the way you judge me and Lenny. Get off my corner. I need to get back to work!" she spews, her hatred reflected in her unfocused eyes.

"Not this time, Annie. This time you are going to hear what I have to say, you may not care or even hear but my conscience won't let me stand by and watch what is happening. I'm shocked to hear that you and Len believe that it is OK for you to do drugs as you try to live up to your responsibilities as parents. I know it is hard and awkward for you to talk to me about what is really going on. You must know that I am trying to get through to you as your friend. Please, Annie, let me arrange for a counselor to meet with you."

She snorts at me and shuffles down the street a little, turns around and shuffles her way back, waves her finger at me in a threatening manner. She tries to laugh but it sounds more like a gurgle.

You need help. I'm telling you if you continue down this road you are going to lose custody of your children. Both you and Len are time bombs waiting to go off and if he goes off on you, it will be terrifying for your kids and heaven only knows what the physical damage will be to you. If you lose it and do something terrible to Len, it will still end in disaster. Both of you are playing with the lives of your two sweet kids. You, as their mother, owe them more. You need help Annie. You're in too deep to be able to crawl out from under this by yourself. I will ask one more time: please let me get a counselor to call you. Just take one call and if that won't work for you, I promise I won't ask again. But do not think I will not watch out for your children and if I believe you are continuing this self- destructive lifestyle, I will contact children's services myself.

This time she tries to take a run at me, slurring with some colourful expletives. "Hah", she finally gets out, "justryansee whatll happntayou!" She gives me the finger and, trying to look fearsome, she weaves back and forth staring once again with her unfocused eyes.

"You owe your children a calm and loving atmosphere. What I see is chaos and fear and that is totally unacceptable. You are a mother and that is the most important message here. You have no right to bring drugs and uncertainty into their lives. You know, too, that you can always come and talk with Gipp. He is available to you anytime he is free. So, tell me, Annie, what is it going to be? Will you take a call from a counselor or not? Think carefully on how you answer." I am tremendously upset with her casual dope-induced lethargic attitude.

Annie holds her head in her hands. She is struggling to keep her eyes focused and seems to nod off for a second or two. She studies her hands and sets them carefully on her lap. She opens her mouth as if she is about to say something but closes it saying nothing. She pushes her sleeve up to scratch at something on her arm and for the first time I see track marks where she has been shooting up. My stomach roils. She looks up at me and tries with some success to look directly at me. Finally, she does say something.

"KOK," she concedes. "I'll take the call but no promises. If I don't like what she says, I won't take another one. She mumbles, I struggle to understand.

Still trembling, I quietly respond but loud enough for her to hear me. "Thank you, Annie. I will call you tomorrow when you are sober and in the right frame of mind to understand. I will pass on her information then. I will arrange for your first visit so you won't need to worry about that, the first contact you have will be to find a day that works for you both. Mark my words, Annie, I am not making empty threats here. I will make that call to children's services if I hear that your children are not being protected as they deserve. I am doing all of this to help you because I love you and I know you have the strength to come through this, whatever it takes. I am proud of you and I do know at this point you probably hate me, but I can't stand by and watch who you are disappear into that dark void. Good night, Annie. Please take my call tomorrow. I will phone in the morning around eleven. "I step toward her, hoping she will let me give her a hug. No such luck.

Weaving, slurring "I'll take your freaking call and I will take the counselor's call, but that's all I am promising you right now. You don't know crap. You think that just because I let you into my life before, I am going to do it again. You've got another thing coming. You come down here pretending to be my friend and all you do is make threats against me. I don't ever want to see your sorry ass again and you can keep your crummy gift bags full of cheap cologne and crappy candies and take your little card and shove it where the sun doesn't shine. You and I are done, you hear me, done!" She spews her venom and walks away. I don't know what is keeping her upright. I can barely discern what she says.

Annie does take my call in the morning and she promises to call the counselor. I can do no more. There is no point in me trying to follow up with her as it is obvious that she wants nothing to do with me right now. I am bereft by what I now know. I know the counselor will not give me any information, so I wait.

* * *

I don't approach Annie for a few weeks. I am hoping she is in counseling and getting the help she needs. I see her each week and her appearance has improved. I don't know if she is still on drugs. I wait for her to approach me when she is ready—if ever! I miss talking with her. I keep track of what is happening on the home front through my talks and meetings with Sarah. Every now and then, I join her and the children on their playdates in the park.

November 1, 2016

A few weeks later, I am sound asleep when my phone rings at 1 a.m. What in the world can this be about? I wonder. Please God, don't let it be bad news.

"Hello," I mumble, still very groggy from being awakened from a sound sleep. This better not be a wrong number. It is freaking only one A.M.!

"Donna, it's Sarah. I'm at Annie's and there's real trouble here. Can you come over right now! Please.

"Of course. Are Annie and the children OK? I ask, getting out of bed.

"The kids are OK; they're asleep. It's Annie and Lenny. They have had a terrible fight. Annie's hurt. I sent Lenny away and told him not to come back. I thought for a minute he was going to hit me, but he stormed out and said he was coming back and that I better not try and stop him. I didn't hear them until Annie called out to me. I'm afraid, Donna. I don't want to be caught in the middle of this mess."

"I know, Sarah. You need to call the police right now and get them involved. I'll get dressed and come right over."

"She won't let me call the police, Donna. She says it is as much her fault as Lenny's. I don't know what to do. I don't want her or Lenny mad at me. I'll wait till you get here and you can make that decision." She hung up.

"*Great,*" I think to myself. "*Put it on me.*" I grab some clothes and wash and change in the bathroom. I am out the door in less than 10 minutes. Twenty minutes later I am knocking on Annie's door. Sarah answers.

"I'm so glad you're here so I can go back to my own apartment," she says. "I will check in the morning and make certain the kids are taken care of. I'll pick them up and we'll go to the park. That will give Annie a chance to recoup and figure out what she wants to do. I can't thank you enough for coming over, I need to go home and get some sleep." Just like that, she is gone, and I am standing in the middle of chaos, once again."

"Look at you, Annie. This time I am calling the police. I am surprised no one in the complex hasn't done so already. You two must have made quite a racket, as I look at the mess you have left in this room. Beer bottles upended, an ash tray filled to the brim, soaked with some kind of fluid. A kitchen chair upended. Let's hope your kids didn't hear anything. Did anyone check to make certain they are asleep? Don't bother telling me not to call the police—you need to get a record of this."

I dial 911 and give the details and my name. I ask for someone to attend right away. I hang up the phone, thanking the person on the other end of the line for their help.

"You have no right to do that!" Annie yells.

"As your friend, I absolutely do. Keep it down Annie! Have you looked in the mirror? You are a mass of bruises, not to mention the split lip. Did you lose any teeth? You have to try and stop this charade. You can argue all you want about what a great dad he is, defend his unwillingness to take a job any job that would help you. You keep insisting this is as much your fault as his. That's garbage Annie, it is not your fault that he is a bully. I believe a man who lays his hands on any woman in violence is a coward who should be in therapy or locked up. You need help Annie from a professional counselor."

I sit next to Annie and put my arms around her as I speak quietly to her. A knock on the door tells me the police have arrived. I get up to let them in.

"Did someone from here call the police? The officer asks.

"Yes, I did. As you can see from Annie's face, this is a case of domestic violence. She and her husband, Len, got into an argument, resulting once again in physical violence." I relate what I believe happened to Annie as best I can.

"You look pretty beat up," the officer says to Annie. "You want to tell me what happened?"

She crosses her arms in front of her, and glares at me. "It was my fault; I was upset when I came home from work and Lenny was drinking with his buddies. They were playing cards and making a lot of noise and most of them were drunk, including Lenny. I was tired and cranky and laid into him about how lazy and useless he is. I kicked his friends out. Lenny got mad and started to yell back at me, getting right in my face. I shoved him and he grabbed me by my arm. He was hurting me, and I slapped at his face and then he just lost it. I know he didn't mean to do this; he'll be sorry when he comes home and sees what he did. It was my fault; I should have handled it better. I should have just gone to bed and talked to him about it in the morning. I told Donna not to call you. I'm sorry we bothered you." I swear she blurted everything out without taking a breath.

"Well, now, ma'am ... he has no right to hit you at all. There is no excuse for a man to lay hands on a woman, no matter the circumstances. Your friend said this is not the first time. Is that correct?" he asks.

She's gesturing wildly and desperate to convince the officer. "Yes, but again it was me getting in his face, yelling, and nagging him for things he is trying to do better. I know he didn't mean for this to happen; he always cries and tells me how sorry he is when he comes back home. Lenny is a good man. It's just so many things are going on that he can't control. No matter how hard he tries, he can't get the job he wants. I know he wants to help me pay the rent and bills, but he can't do that when he can't get a job. He helps me with the children, he does some stuff around here, and he looks after them when I go out to work. My job is a night shift, so it helps that I don't have to pay someone to come in and look after them when I go to work. I am not going to lay charges. I don't even think he will come home tonight, and he certainly won't hurt me again. I know he will feel bad and will be gentle and kind and help me clean up. Thank you though for coming out and offering to help me, but I have made up my mind I will not lay charges against Lenny. So now you can leave." She says in a huff.

The Officer is relaxed and speaks directly to Annie. His voice is quiet and sympathetic. "If you refuse to lay charges then I can't do anything to help you. I can try to find him and talk with him and ensure he doesn't do this again. We find that most men who beat up their spouses do it again and again. He obviously cannot control his temper and that puts you and your children at risk. If I can't convince you that we can and we will provide you with protection, then there is nothing more I can do for you tonight. Would you like me to pick him up and talk to him? I can let him know how badly he has hurt you and that he is leaving himself open to charges and likely going to jail if he does it again. We are here to help you, Annie, and we try to ensure we leave you with a sense of safety, but we can't do that without your cooperation. I need to be sure you do want us to leave and not pursue your husband and take him into custody at least for tonight."

The officer is concerned and is trying hard to help Annie, but I can see he is talking to deaf ears. She is not having any of what he is proposing. I feel helpless and it takes all my willpower not to jump in and offer my advice and tell them I know Len will do this again. I am both angry and terrified for Annie. We are all helpless without Annie's cooperation. Finally, the police leave, and it is just Annie and me in the room.

"Let's get you cleaned up, Annie. You must be exhausted. I know I am. Do you have a first-aid kit and some Tylenol?"

She moves away from me, still annoyed. "Yes, in the bathroom medicine chest there's stuff. I can do this myself, Donna. You can go home. I don't need you here to babysit me. And don't you ever call the police on me again. That was humiliating for me. I don't need any more of you or Sarah interfering in my business. I can look after myself, thank you very much!" she snarls.

It is all I can do to control my own anger at her attitude. I feel put upon and speak sharply.

"Fine. Next time, I'll tell Sarah to let him beat on you until you need hospitalization or worse. Oh, and wait, the children will be here and that will be a life-learning lesson on what not to do in a relationship. And maybe they will even be able to get help for you. What a great experience that will be for them. Well, guess what, we won't let that happen. They are our only concern right now. It is apparent all you and Len care about are yourselves, your drugs, and your booze. Heaven help us if you run out of fuel to pour on the flames once you two go at it. I know I am being sarcastic and pull back, reminding myself she is hurt and scared. Now please, just sit still while I clean you up and then you can go to bed, I can go home, and in the morning you and, hopefully, maybe Len, will help you clean up the mess you have made in the apartment. I am feeling sorry for myself and annoyed she is annoyed with me. I do try to be gentle as I clean her scrapes, but I am very tired, and I let my own feelings rear up.

I am frustrated. "Try and remember Sarah is taking your children on a playdate in the park. Again, you obviously think that, too, is an intrusion into your life but, hey, maybe you could at least thank her when she brings them home. There! You look a lot better. I am sure both your eyes will be black in the morning, your lip looks better, but it will be swollen, so you should look good for your kids and oh, yeah, your job. Good night, Annie. You're welcome. Call me sometime and let me know how you are doing. Maybe you could give some thought to booting Len out before this happens again. By the way, did the counselor get in touch with you?" Sarcasm oozes.

"Yes, and I have been to see her twice since then. I have another appointment next week. I'm sorry, Donna. I know you are just trying to help, but you need to understand I can look after myself and you and Sarah just make it harder for me to deal with Lenny when you come here and try and take over. Lenny feels threatened by you guys and it just upsets him more when you get involved. We both just want is best for our children. I keep telling you both how good he is with them and I know in my heart he will never lash out at them. He only lashes at me when I get on his case. I need to learn to back off and give him some space. He is under such a lot of stress; I don't know why he can't find a job. He made an honest, good living at it when we lived in Prince Albert. I know that once he gets that job, he'll do well, and all this stuff will go away. Maybe you could help him find a job, Donna, she pleads. "You know lots of people."

Wearily I respond. "I do, Annie but I don't know any in car repairs or mechanics. Why doesn't he take something else until the one he wants comes along? That would relieve a lot of the stress from you both. He can't keep drinking and doing drugs and expect to find any job let alone the one he wants. I am too tired to do this now, it's late and I need to go home and get some sleep. Try and get some rest, Annie. I'll put some milk in the microwave while you get ready for bed, you can take that with one of your pills. The warm milk will settle your tummy down and help you to sleep. I would lock your doors so that Len can't get in tonight. I suggest you change the locks so just you have a key and that way he can only come in when you allow it. You at least will have some control over your home front. Just a suggestion.

Annie has changed into her pajamas, hesitantly walks to the microwave. Without acknowledging me she takes the milk out of the microwave.

Please, please don't let Len back in here tonight. It is almost 4 A.M., so I would assume he has crashed elsewhere. Keep in touch and I'll see you Thursday night. If you need to go to a doctor about your ribs, let me know and I will make the time to take you. Good night, Annie. I love you. You need to remember that—and Sarah loves you, too." I reach to hug her, but she jerks away. I leave, closing the door gently but I want to slam it, open it and slam it shut again, but I don't.

November 2, 2016

Once again, my phone rings, waking me. I peer at my clock it is 9 a.m. I feel as if I have just gotten into my bed. The ringing is incessant. I reach over and pick up the phone, more to shut it up than to find out who is on the other end of it.

"Hallo!" I answer angrily.

"Donna, it's Annie. Could you please come over right now? Nothing is wrong. I am fine. I would just like to share a cup of coffee with you. Please come, Donna, it's important." She sounds desperate.

"What's going on? You don't sound like everything is OK. I'm very tired, Annie. As you know, none of us got much sleep last night. Can you wait a couple of hours?" I ask, still feeling as if I am half asleep.

"I really need you to come now, Donna. It really is important. I wouldn't ask if it wasn't," she pleads.

"Can Sarah help you for now and I promise I'll come as soon as I've had more sleep."

"Please come now, Donna. I can't explain over the phone, but I need you now! Please!"

"All right, Annie. I will be there in 15 minutes," I acquiesce when I really don't want to.

It takes me half an hour to finally get there.

"Annie, I hope this is as urgent as you made it sound," I say as she answers my knock on her door.

I follow her into the kitchen and Len is sitting at the table, looking furious.

I am stunned to see him here. "What is this all about Annie—and why are you here, Len? I have no intention of getting into any kind of a conversation with you. I said all I am going to say the last time you confronted me. I am here as Annie's friend; I am not here to interfere with the two of you. She sounded scared and desperate on the phone. Looking at you, I assume you are the reason for that. Now, one of you please tell me what is going on right now or I am turning around and going out that door." Inside, I am seething.

Submissively, Annie looks at me. "Please Donna, sit and I'll get you a cup of coffee. Lenny's here this early because he wants to know why the police were here and why did I call them. Please tell him it wasn't me who called them and that I defended him to them."

Flabbergasted, I reply "You're kidding me, is this why you called me waking me up? Lenny, you could have asked me over the phone and Annie if he refused you could have called later in the day. I don't know why can't you see how difficult you are making it for me or anyone else to help you? It is hard for me to stand by and watch him hurt you physically and having to watch you deal with his baggage as well as your own. I am watching you drown emotionally with all the stress, fear and responsibility resulting in situations like this. I am pretty tired myself right now, and Len, I beg you to stop making Annie's life so damn hard. Surely you can see what you are doing to her. Is this too much to ask of you? Don't you think it's sad that she believes she has to call on me to get your approval and understanding that she did not make that call for help?" I plop down on a chair, weary of it all.

Len stands over me and snarls. "You're damn right she called you to straighten this all out. You got no business coming here and making trouble for me and my family. Who do you think you are?" He is already raising his voice.

Wearily I respond with as much authority as I can muster up. "I came to help Annie. She was hurt and afraid after you beat her up. And yes, I did call the police and yes Annie did not want me to, but someone must take steps to stop you bullying your way in here and beating on her just because she asks you some pretty, legitimate questions. You are bleeding her dry. Take a good look at her, Len. She is skin and bones, she's terrified of you, enough to get me to come over and defend my actions and make certain you know it was me and not her who called them. What would you have done Len, beat her again? If I had my way, you would have been arrested and charged and prayerfully sent to jail for a long time. Annie refused to lay charges this time, but no doubt there will be a next time because that's the only way you know how to fix things. I am wound up now running on fumes.

"How do you look at yourself in the mirror knowing you beat on a defenseless woman who is half your size, thin as a rail, and totally helpless against your fists? It's disgusting. *When,* because I know it's not *if* you touch her again, you can be sure I will call the cops and I am certain you know this that each time they are called to a partner violence it is logged. You are now on their radar, so you might want to think twice about hitting her again."

I spew my words, leaning on the edge of the table and trying hard to get in his face. I am furious at them both for hauling me back into their crappy relationship.

He takes a step toward me. "You stupid bitch, you got no right to talk to me like this," Len says. "You can't tell me how to handle my family. If you keep interfering, I will get children's services involved and let them know what she does to earn money and that half of what she earns goes into her arm and up her nose. Who do you think will get custody of our kids? You can be damn sure it won't be her and it won't matter a damn what you have to say about it. So, keep your nose out of my business or Annie will be the one to suffer the consequences. His face has taken on a purplish hue, he seems to be vibrating as he continues with his rant.

"You don't know what really goes on here, you only know what she tells you! Half of what she tells you is bull—you think she doesn't get some of those bruises on her arms and stomach from her 'dates'? Len stands and leans on the table. I can smell his sweat, and believe full well that if I were Annie, he would punch me in the face, his anger is that palpable.

I take a step back, afraid to get in his face and attempt to tone it down. "You know, Len, I never come here to speak with you without being invited to do so. It is extremely upsetting for me to contend with your verbal abuse. I come, always hoping I can help both of you come to a peaceful coexistence that could work for all of you. I don't claim to have any formal training and my intentions are always full of peaceful expectations. I am embarrassed about my loss of control. From now on I believe it will be best if I only come here when you are not here." Annie finally steps in between us and meekly says. "Donna you should go, I'm sorry I called you, but I needed Lenny to know I didn't call the cops and I will never do that. I called you because I needed help and I was scared. You don't have a right to talk to Lenny like this. You are not being fair; he was only defending himself. I need both of you to go so I can settle down before Sarah and the kids come back from their park date. Please try to understand, Donna, that Lenny doesn't mean to hurt me. I need to back off and try to understand what it is like for him not to be able to support his family the way he always has. Isn't that right Lenny? Thanks for coming over Donna and I'm sorry he said all those things to you. Are we still friends?"

I am astonished, and wonder if she will ever really understand the danger, she is in. "Of course, Annie. But I can't abide you, Len. You know that I know exactly who you are and that I will be here for her doing my best to get her help. I pray you will soon find work and will be able to help her financially. I'll see you Thursday night, Annie. Please take care of yourself. I turn and snap at Len. After you, Lenny—you heard Annie she wants both of us out of here now!"

We both leave together. I can almost feel him vibrating with animosity and rage as we walk out of the apartment building.

November 30, 2016

The past few weeks have been quiet on the streets. It is cold, dark and windy tonight. Sunny has been her usual erratic self. I really enjoy interacting with her. She is a sweet woman under all that tough exterior. A couple of weeks ago, Darcy, her best friend from the streets was found dead. She is still broken up about it and is acting out. I feel her pain. She and Darcy were inseparable, always together. She was deep into the drug trade and I guess that lifestyle just got to be too much for her. My heart aches for these girls, when they go through sorrow, pain, and chaos. I hear many people say it is their choice to do what they do, but most, who sit in judgment of them have no idea what puts them here. Some come to earn enough money to feed their children. Circumstances are different for everyone, but each one has a story—sad, hopeless, and it often goes back to an abusive childhood, domestic violence, or simply a poor choice. At times, they have been recruited from high schools, given promises of an exciting lifestyle, parties, friendships etc. Ninety percent of the time the recruiter gets them hooked on drugs and the girls are forced to pay for them by doing what the recruiter says. Others choose it. As I say, each one has a story, and it is not my place to judge. I have a deep and abiding love for each one and my heart breaks when their hearts get broken for whatever reason.

I visit with Sunny for a few minutes, spot Misty, stop and visit, give her a hug and a gift bag, and head over to Annie's corner.

"Looking good, Annie. Things are still going well for you and the kids?" I ask, giving her one of my gift bags. She is pale and very thin. She has put on some makeup and she is well groomed. Her outfit is cute, she has on black leggings with a white hoodie, and a nice pink scarf. Her boots are scuffed, but they look comfortable. She has put on a wide pink headband trying unsuccessfully to keep her unruly curls in control.

She wavers a little and gives me a hesitant smile. "Yeah, things are really good with Lenny now. He looks after the kids for four hours in the day while I do a shift in the small coffee shop around the corner from us. I don't know what I'd do without him. The kids adore him, and he is good with them. I'm really lucky he is willing to help out." She slurs her words.

She is obviously high, but I don't say anything tonight. I keep praying Len will get out of her life or that she opens her eyes and sees what we, her friends, see. Frankly, I find it frustrating to listen to her talk glowingly about him. I have seen the soft side of him when he is with his children, but I have also seen the results of his brutality. To my knowledge, he pays nothing toward rent, food, or any of the other normal expenses most partners share. She is blind to his faults. It is ridiculous that she believes it is OK for her to work two jobs while he does not work at all. She continues to applaud him for looking out for their children while she wears herself out keeping their heads above water each month. I keep these thoughts and my feelings to myself.

For tonight, I chat with her and listen to her. I know Sarah is keeping an eye out and will let me know if she notices things escalating. What is obvious to me is that Annie is on a downward spiral that she won't be able to hide much longer. The more I watch her, the more alarm bells go off in my head. I am frightened for her. Her health is deteriorating, her emotions are erratic, and she is losing weight at an alarming rate.

"You're losing a lot of weight Annie. Are you feeling OK?

She narrows her eyes like she is suspicious of why I am asking any questions. "I know. I am trying to lose some—I was having some problems getting into my clothes and I don't want to buy new ones because I can't afford to do that. It costs me enough just trying to keep my kids in clothes. Besides, if I don't control my weight, nothing will fit me. I feel great, though. I haven't been this healthy since I left Prince Albert, so that is a good thing. You worry too much, Donna. Things are good with me and Lenny, the kids are happy, and all is well with us." She rattles her answer and quickly asks. "How about you? You're looking a little tired these days. Are you trying to do too much?

I know you work a lot with some of the other women. Maybe you should take some time off, take a trip, or just laze around your house for a few weeks. We'll be OK out here. You know we all look out for each other when we are on a date. There haven't been any bad dates for at least a month. I haven't heard of any, have you?"

Wow, she turned that conversation on me, successfully putting the focus on my needs. She looks frail. She stands erect and almost on guard. She looks as if she is inwardly challenging me to say something negative.

I lower my eyes and chuckling I respond to her questions.

"No, it's been pretty quiet, but we know that can change in a heartbeat. You don't need to worry about me, Annie. I am just fine. I certainly don't need to take any time to hang around my home doing nothing. I have lots that I do that relaxes me and takes my mind off any of the things that tend to get me in a tizzy. Anyway, I'm glad you are keeping well. She looks like she is tuning me out. "Put some meat on those bones or soon you'll have to buy smaller clothes and that will be even worse. We all know it is always easier to put weight on. I'm going to head home; you stay safe tonight and be sure and contact me if you need anything."

Annie is not going to say any more. She seems almost bored.

"Remember, I can always give you gift cards from Save-On-Foods. You don't need to do without food at any time. That is part of this ministry. Remember, God loves you and so do I. Take good care, dear one. I'll see you next Thursday."

I am close to tears by the time I get home, I am so worried about Annie. I know she is using, and I can't do anything to help until she admits she needs it. For the first time, I am desperate, I know she could lose custody of her children. I pray to my God that He will watch over her and her children.

January 17, 2017

It is some weeks later when I get a call from Sarah. She tells me she is very worried about Annie. Jessie, Annie's daughter, rushed over and said his mommy wouldn't wake up. Sarah is afraid to go over in case she is dead. She won't call the police or 911 in case Len finds out. She is afraid of him and has told me several times she won't call so he won't come after her for getting the police involved.

"Don't be afraid Sarah. I'm on my way, but you need to reassure those children that their mom is just sleeping. I have a feeling she has overdosed, or she is just so worn out she is unwilling to get up. At least go over and get the kids something to eat. Put the kettle on for tea; I could use a cup and I am sure Annie will want some when we get her up. I'm on my way now, I have my cellphone with me. I will be there in 10 minutes."

When Sarah answers the door to Annie's apartment, I can see she is in a terrible state. Her hands are shaking so badly she can barely hug me. The children are on the floor, sitting in front of the TV watching cartoons. They each have a bowl of dry, sweetened cereal and are laughing at something they are watching. I close the door quietly and slip into Annie's bedroom.

It is apparent there is something seriously wrong with her. She is white as a ghost and barely breathing. There is nothing we can do to help except to call 911. I pull out my cell phone and place the call; I give them my name and give them what information I am able. They assure me they will be there in less than five minutes.

I rush into the kitchen and ask Sarah to take the children over to her apartment so I can deal with the paramedics when they arrive. She agrees immediately. We both know what distress the children will experience if they see their mother being administered to by the medics. It is all *we* can do not to panic.

"OK guys, enough TV, let's all go to the park and get some ice cream after. First one to grab their jacket and get over to my place wins an extra swing at the park."

They all dash off, grab jackets, and are out the door faster than the speed of lightning, I swear. It is so good to see that kind of excitement. I wonder if Annie realizes what a fantastic neighbor she has. Sarah is an amazing person, and she has a lot of love for Annie's children. My heart overflows with love for her. I give her a big hug and no sooner does her door shut than I hear the ambulance arriving, sirens blaring. Thank heavens the children won't see them enter their home.

"Did you call for an ambulance?" the paramedic asks as she sees me standing in front of the open door to Annie's. She's tall and slim. Her dark hair is cut in layers and shows off her pretty face. She has dark eyes and her olive complexion show a trace of Asian descent. She is kind and friendly.

"Yes, I did. My name is Donna, if you follow me, I will show you where Annie is. She appears to have over-dosed; she is breathing but may be unconscious." I frantically relate.

She shakes my hand. "Hi, my names Rita." she follows me to where Annie is.

She examines Annie. "How long has she been like this?" she asks.

I take a deep breath and try to gather my wits about me. "Her neighbor said she had left her apartment after they shared a cup of coffee. She had agreed to take care of the children after Annie fed them lunch so Annie could take a nap as she was exhausted. It was no more than 15 minutes after she had left with her children that Annie's daughter ran back to Sarah's, telling her that her mommy wouldn't wake up. Sarah immediately called me, and it took me 15 minutes to get here so, maybe half an hour. Sarah left with the children just as you arrived. Is Annie going to be okay?" I can't stop shaking.

"Yes, she's coming around. Do you know if she is using drugs?"

"Yes, I know she is. I'm not sure what she is taking but as you can see, she is very thin, and she has been losing weight steadily for about two months now—oh! I realize Annie is awake.

Like always I start to interrogate her. "Annie, are you OK? You scared us all. What did you do?" I fire questions at her.

Rita gently pats my arm and gently moves me aside. "Take it easy, let me ask the questions. She will be a bit groggy for a while. We are going to take her into the hospital and once she is stable, she'll probably need to go into rehab. We will contact children's services so her kids will be cared for."

I immediately go on the defensive. "No, you don't need to do that. I'll get in touch with Len; he's her husband and the children's dad. He can come and care for them. He is not home right now, but I have a number where I can reach him. He lives here and looks after his children while Annie works. I'll make sure he is here and understands he will need to be here 24 hours a day until Annie returns."

I am talking a mile a minute, trying my best to ensure the paramedic does not call children's services. I send a text to Len and tell him to get over here right away or his children are going to be placed in foster care today.

Like a blind pulled down over a window, the shutter goes down over her eyes. "We can't just leave without being sure the children are in the care of a relative or you can assure us that you will care for them until Annie is ready to come home." She gets a nod from the other paramedic.

Fortunately, Len answers my text and tells me he is on his way home. I show it to both paramedics, and they are good with that. They take Annie out and are gone when Len arrives.

He rushes into the apartment frantically firing questions at me. "What the hell is going on? What happened to Annie? Is she OK? Where are the kids?" His hair is disheveled, his jacket collar is twisted, shoelaces are untied.

"Take it easy Len, the children are at the park with Sarah. They won't be home for at least another hour. She is taking them for lunch and ice cream when they leave the park. They are in good hands. Annie is being taken to the hospital as we speak. I don't know exactly what happened. She seemed exhausted we just couldn't wake her up. I have no idea what's going on. As you know, she's burning the candle at both ends, working in the afternoon and most of the night. She probably doesn't take the time to eat properly, and certainly is not getting enough rest, it is no wonder she finally collapsed under the stress. You will need to talk to the hospital to get all the details." I am quite worried that I will slip up and say more than I should. I don't want to be the one to tell him about her drug use. For all I know, she is being treated for something by her doctor and she had a negative reaction to the medicine. I just know I don't want to be the one in the middle. I know how popular heroin is and pray silently they put her into detox.

He sits down and puts his head in his hands, shaking it back and forth. "I bet she's taking something she shouldn't be. She's always accusing me of snorting coke and drinking too much. I bet she's gone and overdosed and now she's in it up to her neck. Once children's services find out about this, I will be the one to have custody of my kids. She doesn't deserve to have them if she is so irresponsible.

What if you or Sarah hadn't been here to get help for my kids, what do you think would have happened? Where would they have gone or how could they have got help right away?" he moaned.

I slump down beside him. "Maybe you should give them your phone number so they can get a hold of you. You must take some responsibility for what is going on with Annie. Please don't judge her, no matter what happened here, Len. You need to step up and help her.

He snatches it away and leaps out of his chair. "Don't you put this on me, Donna. She knows all she needs to do is call me and I will come and take the kids or do whatever she needs. I have been at her beck and call for the last six weeks. You have no idea what I have been through with her, nagging and pulling at me. I am in the middle of getting welfare, so I will be able to help with money soon and she knows that. I can't believe you never knew she was using; she is not just losing weight; she is a mess. She is all over the place, yelling, and screaming about this and that, not making any sense. The kids are scared half the time to go near her, she is so erratic. Maybe it's a good thing this happened. They'll make her go into detox and maybe she stays straight after. Who knows?" He kicks at a chair sending it sailing.

I stand feeling defeated. "Well, let's hope she gets the help she needs. You need to take some responsibility too, Len. I have seen you drunk and so have your kids so don't go preaching on what a lot of sacrifices you've had to make. You can come and go as you please, Annie has no alternative except to be here, needs to make sure she can pay the rent, buy the groceries, make sure the children have the clothes they need, and all the other things required. Anyway, I am going home, you can call me if you need anything, particularly if the children are in distress. As well, you know Sarah is right across the hall. I am sure she will continue with their playdates, so that will free you up somewhat. In the meantime, please let me know where Annie is and what her prognosis is. Let's let the doctors do what they do and if they put her in detox, just work with them and her to make sure she recovers enough to stay off the stuff once she is released. I really hope that for your children's sake that you will do everything to help her make this transition as easy as possible for her.

I'm out of here. Thanks for answering my text right away, Len. I was afraid they were going to call children's services and then Lord only knew when and how we would have gotten them back. Take good care, Len."

I go home and collapse on my couch. I am truly in a conundrum. I must admit from what Len was telling me it appears he has been the one looking after things. She is the one who is dropping the ball. If she doesn't get clean and sober, she is going to lose custody of her children. Even though Len has been stepping up, I wonder if he is still using as well as drinking way too much to be able to care for the children. I need to take a nap; my brain is really fuzzy right now and I am exhausted with worry for Annie.

January 18, 2017

I am groggy. I must have fallen asleep on the couch. I blearily look at my watch and see I have been sleeping for two hours. As the fog in my head clears, I begin to put the hours before together. I am anxious to know where Annie is and whether she will be permitted to have visitors. I am worried about her children but also wary about interfering with Len. I get up and make myself a cup of coffee, hoping that will clear my mind. I decide to call the hospital first and then I plan to phone Sarah and find out what happened when she dropped the kids off to Len.

The hospital is not forthcoming, as I am not a family member. They tell me she is being observed and consultations are taking place to determine their best course of action.

I am anxious for Annie for what she will have to face to get her life back on track. I call several of my friends and ask them to lift her up in prayer. I am committed to helping her get her life back on track. We need to get more professional help for her. I have some funds in the ministry for this purpose. She need never know from where the funds come.

March 3, 2017

Annie was in detox for six weeks. She called me the day of her release and I went to pick her up. She looks so good I am moved to tears to see how clear her eyes shine. She has gained some weight and she looks happy, so much like the young woman I first saw on the streets. I pray to my God that we can encourage and support her enough that she will be able to stay clean and sober.

"Hi, Annie! You look terrific!" I hug her to me and tell her I love her and am thrilled to see her.

I hand her the bag of clothes I picked up from her apartment on my way here.

She quickly dresses and signs all the required paper-work, we leave and walk to my car, chattering as we go.

"Oh Donna! It's so good to be out of there. It was hard for me to be away from my kids. I'm glad I am clean now and I'm going to stay clean, I promise. That was difficult for me, Donna—you have no idea how hard it is to detox. I felt like I was going to die, the pain and the sick feeling that was unrelenting. I couldn't eat for days. I can't ever go through that again. Promise me you'll never put me in that place again, Donna. It is inhumane what they put me through!" she wails.

Here we go again I am the scape goat. "I can't make that promise, Annie. It was not me who put you in that position, it was you. The drugs finally took hold of you and you are lucky to be alive. You have got to remember what all of that was like. Not just for you but for your children, Len, Sarah, me, and the paramedics who attended to you. You should be grateful, Annie, and your fear of detoxing again could well keep you off the drugs. It is totally up to you what direction you choose. Len has done a great job of looking after your children, along with Sarah's help. If the situation between you and Len is still toxic, you are going to have to deal with it in a way that works for you and your children. There are two people who deal with this kind of situation who are on tap to take you on as a client. There is no cost to you, and I recommend that you accept their help. In the meantime, let's get you home so you can see and be with your children again. They are excited to see you, Annie. They were bouncing off the walls when I stopped in to get some clothes for you and I told them you were coming home."

"Me too," she said. "I am anxious to see them; it seems like such a long time since I held them and hugged them and told them myself how much I love them. It is archaic to believe it is in the children's best interest that they are not allowed to stay with their moms. I don't believe that, it is not as if we are spaced out. In fact, I know for myself my recovery would have been much quicker had I had my children with me. Anyway, it is over now, and I am finally where I want to be." She leaps out of the car and runs to the elevator. I am left to get her luggage. She and the elevator have long gone when I finally lock the car and walk over to it. I push the call button and wait for its return. I am happy for Annie and her family, but I want to go home to my own life now. When I get to her apartment, there are gleeful shouts and tears. Mother and children hug one another. I drop off everything that I had retrieved from my car, yell goodbye, and leave them to their joyful reunion.

The next few weeks are uneventful. I see Annie every Thursday night and she looks well and happy. We chat briefly and she discloses little information other than to tell me she is doing great and everything is going well with Len and their children. It is a relief for me to know she is keeping off all chemicals and is maintaining her weight. I hear from Sarah every now and then and she reiterates what Annie tells me, so I can relax and deal with my own life and be more available to the other women with whom I am involved.

A few weeks after her release from detox, Annie comes down with a particularly serious case of the flu. She is very, ill, and Sarah and I are basically on call. During this time, I watch Len take over all the necessary duties required to keep a family functioning. I must admit to myself that he is a great dad and seemingly devoted husband. For the first time, I am forced to think about my attitude toward him. I am seeing the man Annie so often describes to me and I am compelled to believe he was a good and decent man when they first married and for five years after that. I wonder what happened to change him so drastically. I know the drugs and alcohol abuse are the surface causes, but what was the underlying chaos that led him to bury himself in such a self-destructive way.

I carry a sadness in my heart knowing how he behaved once he moved into Annie's apartment. I wonder how he hides it all so well at times like this when his family is in crisis. I am hopeful the animosity he and Annie experienced will lessen and they will be able to work out an amicable arrangement resulting in a peaceful coexistence. Not only is Annie quite ill, but both their children are ill as well, and yet he carries on and ensures their needs and more are being met. Sarah and I help with laundry and we often provide at least one meal a day. During the three weeks of their illnesses, I never saw any evidence that Len was either drinking or using drugs. He was always very attentive and caring toward them all. It was really something to see. And he never got ill himself. I certainly had to change all the negative thoughts I had nurtured in my own mind about who he was. Nevertheless, I could not ignore the times we saw the results of his physical and mental abuse aimed at Annie.

I hear many people believe that sometimes the woman deserves and even causes the violent behavior aimed at them, but that can never be the accepted reason for any man to lay hands on a woman in anger. I realize that some abused women, including Annie, will say it was their fault, they caused the anger rise to rage, and that is what made the man to lose his temper and lash out physically. I believe the abused partner is so verbally beaten down by their abuser they assume it is their fault. This too, can never be an accepted reason for violence. I was relieved when things got back to, normal in Annie's household.

Gipp and I are going on a cruise in a week, and we will be gone for two weeks. I am excited to get organized and I feel a little panicky at how quickly the time is moving on and how much I still need to do!

I let the women know I will be gone for three weeks, knowing it will take me a week to get back to normal after living the life of luxury on board a cruise ship.

Annie and Len seemed to be doing well. The last time I had coffee with them he told me that he had been to a job interview for a mechanic position and he was positive he would get the job. He seemed happy and excited, as did Annie. I left on that note and had a wonderful time on the cruise. When we returned, I found out that all hell had broken out in Annie's life once again.

April 6, 2017

My first Thursday down on the streets is busy and chaotic. We have two bad dates that we report to the police and a fight between two women: one is so high she can hardly stand and there is a needle embedded in her arm where she last shot up. I calm the fight down and take the woman to the street nurse down in Common Square. I am rattled when I return to the stroll and see Annie. She has two black eyes and looks bedraggled.

"Hi, Annie. You look like you got run over by a truck or at least a fist. What and who happened?"

She stretches as if she is annoyed. "It's nothing, Donna. I slipped and fell against the table and knocked myself out and woke with two black eyes. I am so clumsy, it's a wonder I haven't broken any bones. I feel a little tired; it is taking me longer to get over that flu than I thought it would. I'll be OK. I look worse than if feel, honest." She smiles.

"No, no, Annie. You don't have to lie about what happened. It doesn't take a rocket scientist to notice how you are walking and holding your stomach. Did Len do this or was it a bad date? I put my arms around her and hold her, I can feel her vibrating, and I hear her wince when I hold her close. I release her and stand back while I wait for her to tell me the truth.

Once more her deductions are unreasonable. "It wasn't his fault. It was me and my mouth and I am incredibly clumsy when I get angry. I don't look where I am going. I am so mad I just stumble around, flaying my arms and yelling at Lenny. He has been really, good Donna; he tries hard to help and the kids adore him. He didn't get the job he applied for and he thought for sure that he had aced the interview. He was drinking and using. I told him he had to get that stuff out of the apartment and that he had to take himself out and not come back till he had sobered up. The kids were screaming and crying.

Now the waterworks start. "It was horrible Donna; I don't know who was screaming the loudest, him or me. I said some terrible things to him, and I punched at him first. I missed and he grabbed me and slapped my face. It all got worse from there. We were both trying to hurt each other. He is stronger so I look a lot worse than he does. I did really fall against the table at one point, and I think that's when my ribs got bruised. You can't blame Lenny, Donna. I should have been more sympathetic and at least tried to understand what he was going through, but I got so mad when I saw him drinking since the kids could see what he was doing." I reacted to what I saw. I saw red Donna. She mopped her nose on her sleeve.

She continued her rant. "I just lost it. I swiped the coke off the table, the bottle of hooch, and the drugs all went flying, the bottle broke, and his coke was in the air. He was furious and out of control and that just got me all lit up. We both started hitting and slapping at one and other. I'm sure I was the first to hit him. I called him every crude name I could think of. He retaliated and through a red haze of rage. My little boy tried to get us apart by kicking at his daddy. I'm humiliated: I can hardly look either of them in the eye. They seem so downtrodden. I don't know what to say to them, other than tell them how sorry I am. They ask if their daddy is hurt like I am and ask where he is, if he is in the hospital, or is he dead, and why isn't he home with us. Why did I hurt him and yell at him so loud and why did he hurt me so bad? They are bewildered. I just try to answer as honestly as I can. They are wounded by it all, Donna; it is such a mess." She is pacing, she seems frantic, trying to get control but still seething.

I step back so as not to crowd her. I am concerned she might strike me as she flails her arms angrily. I take some deep breaths and hesitantly try to respond in a way that will help to settle her emotional tirade.

"Oh my gosh, Annie. I am sorry this all happened. Do you know where Len is? Have you heard from him?"

"No." she weeps.

"When did this take place? Who has the children now while you are working? I hope Sarah is still your friend and is taking care of them." I fire these questions, hoping she has the information. I am astonished at what has transpired and frightened for Annie and the children.

Her cries are more like a soft moan now as she gets control.

"I don't know where Lenny is, or if he is hurt. I don't even know where he went. This all happened a week ago. He was distraught when he came home after being told he didn't get the job. I was still tired and didn't feel that great after the flu and snapped at him. I told him to get another job, there were lots of them out there, maybe not what he wanted right now but at least he could be helping more if he just settled for something else right now. I told him I was sick and tired of doing everything while he sat around doing nothing but whining about how hard his life was." She wavers, I reach for her frightened she might faint. She waves me off and steadies herself. "I know I was unfair to him, but I had not had a great day either. The kids had been whining and fighting most of the day and I had just had enough. I started it all Donna; it wasn't his fault. You saw how wonderful he was when I was in detox and how sweet and caring he was when the kids and I were sick. He was positive he would get that job, he talked about how good he had been in the interview, and how encouraging the person who interviewed him had been when he left. When he came home dejected and hurt, I wasn't there for him, I was wrapped up in my own misery so I couldn't give him what he so desperately needed." She is determined to absolve Len.

I take a deep breath, thinking carefully of how to respond. "It'll be OK Annie. We can try to find him and make sure he is OK. Do you have any names of friends where he may have gone? I am sure he landed somewhere

where he would be safe and have time to settle down and come to terms with what happened. Annie, you must stop making excuses for him. It is never okay for him to hit you. What he should do is walk away and leave when you become ballistic. He doesn't seem to know what to do or how to handle you; but under no circumstances does he have the right to physically abuse you.

"It was my fault Donna, aren't you listening?" she blubbers.

"I hear you Annie. You don't have the right to abuse him either. I understand what you are saying about how wrung out you were, but taking it out on him only escalates the violence. It all comes down to one thing Annie: he should move out. Neither of you have any right to allow your children to go through this kind of turmoil. Imagine how they must feel, scared to death one of you is going to kill the other and the words that you both probably spewed out were deplorable. They must have been terrified and felt totally helpless. It's unbelievable that either of you would put them in such an awful situation. Children should never be made to feel helpless and terrified at any time at the hands of their parents or caregivers."

In retrospect I should have stopped there instead I continued as if I was giving Annie a lecture. "They are both going to need a lot of tender care and words that will help them know that neither of you meant any harm to come to each other or to them. That you love them and will never do anything like that or anything that will make them feel unprotected again ever. It will take a lot of nurturing and time to make them feel safe again. They must be your priority, not Len and not yourself. No excuses, Annie. There is never an excuse to allow our emotions to get fired to a point where our children will be witness to abhorrent behavior."

I am angry with both Annie and Len. At the same time, I feel sorrow for Annie because of what she is going through—the guilt, the anguish, and her shame at what had taken place in front of her babies. I can feel her torment. I take her hand and walk her to the steps. We both sit and I let her weep until she finally gathers herself and is able to talk coherently.

Shoulders slumped, her head down she looks bewildered. "What should I do?" What if something terrible has happened to Lenny? I could never forgive myself if he is hurt anywhere and alone with no help. I will make it up to my kids, I will sit them down and answer all their questions honestly and assure them this will never happen again. I can't kick their father out without them believing it is because of the fight we had. I will have to work with Lenny in making things better at home. It is too dangerous for me to have drugs or liquor in our home. I am a recovering addict and I deserve that much consideration for my feelings. I will need to set some written guidelines and he will have to agree to them if he wants to live with us. He is a good man, Donna, and a great dad; he only hits me when I get so mad that I say things that hurt him—and I hit him too. I know I need to curb my temper and use words instead of actions. We both need to harness our rage. Will you help me find Lenny, Donna? Please? We miss him and I am worried he is hurt and alone somewhere," she pleads.

"All those things sound great Annie; I just hope you can put them into action successfully. I don't have the answers; you need to let your psychiatrist know what happened. I don't know how I can help you find Lenny; I have no idea where he would go. I believe you should just wait for him to get in touch with you or he may just show up at home and expect things to be as they were before all of this took place. I will ask around and get Gipp to put the word out on the streets to see if anyone knows him or knows where he is. That is really the best I can do. I am certain that he will come home when he has cooled down and believes all will be forgiven."

I say these words with a sense of dread, not knowing if Len is hurt and if he is, getting help. The thought of him going back home to Annie scares me to death. There is just too much stress and friction between them. After witnessing the wonderful way Len stood up and cared for his children while Annie was in detox and again after; when they all came down with the flu, it is hard for me to envision this same man being this volatile and brutal. I really need to stop thinking this way that.

April 27, 2017

It was two weeks before Len appeared on Annie's doorstep. The following Thursday I met with Annie on the streets. I am flabbergasted at her demeanor.

"Hi, Annie. You look chipper tonight," I say as I hand her a gift bag.

"Oh, Donna, I'm very, excited. Lenny came home last Tuesday. He said how sorry he was, and he promised to never lay a hand on me in anger again. He said he had been talking to a counselor at one of the shelters downtown. He looks so good. He was clean and neatly dressed and so full of love and adoration for our children. He hugged me and told me how much he needed and loved me and that things would be very, different from now on. He was so contrite, I felt sorry for him. You know what I mean. I told him how proud of him I was that he was getting counseling and how I could already see a big change in his attitude.

"We had a wonderful day. We took the kids to the park, had hot dogs and pop at the beach, we all ran around chasing each other like a crazy bunch, and oh it was so

157

much fun. I haven't seen Len like this since about the third year of our marriage. You know what it's like—kids come the job takes up more of your time because you offer to work overtime to keep ahead of expenses. Something must give, doesn't it. I am happier than I have been for a very, long time. I know we can do this. He even promised to take a lower-paying job until he can find one more in his field. It's all going to be okay, Donna."

She is over the moon as she blurts out the excitement that is in her soul.

Me? I am flabbergasted that she has completely forgotten the beating she had taken a little over two weeks ago. It is like she has turned a blind eye to the damage to her children and their terror at how it had all played out. I wonder if she perhaps has a slight case of amnesia. In my mind I can't understand how she can so easily take the same level of responsibility that Len has. How can she so easily forgive all that has taken place and then she welcomes him home like nothing has changed? Once again, Len has returned to the same freedoms he had before this last fiasco. He promised again to take a lesser-paying job, I think to myself, *Yeah, we'll wait to see that happen.* Annie has not made any demands on him; he simply said all the right words like he always has. I feel wretched, knowing she honestly believes his bullying is on her. It is so unfair to Annie. I question his love for her, I see a man who is cruel and selfish. I pray one day Annie will see what I see.

I sit next to Annie on the steps, and I am totally speechless. I am in such turmoil that I struggle with what and how I should react. I am stunned and sit in silence for what seems like an eternity. Annie just sits there with the biggest smile on her face, like she has won the lottery or something. She looks pretty in a little yellow lace top and brown shorts. Her hair is cut short and hugs her face. She has tied a pretty, pale gold ribbon around a small curl. She wears little makeup and tonight her face is glowing with joy. Her sandals are white with little gold buttons on the straps. I am delighted to see her like this, but at the same time I worry for her and her children. I don't know how to describe the whole situation. Finally, I do have something to say.

"Gee, Annie, I am surprised that things are going so well so quickly. Do you remember all that happened that night or have you forgotten how out of control you both were in front of your children?" I keep my voice even and speak softly.

"Of course not, Donna, but Lenny is desolate that he was that out of control. I love him and I am happy he is back home with us.

I am confused and exasperated. "What about the bruises and the agony you went through right after? I'm sorry Annie, but I am having a problem getting all of this wrapped around my head. Surely you don't intend for Len to just walk back into your life with no rules or at least a promise that he gets a job and contributes to the expenses you have been struggling to pay."

I am frightened for her and her children, but I am trying to keep my own emotions in check.

She snorts "You worry too much Donna, the bruises made me look a lot worse than I was. I am totally okay, and I know I exaggerate how bad I am hurt. I'm sorry I scare you. Prince Albert is a long way to come to be with me and the kids."

That information had been niggling in the back of my mind. "By the way, how did he find out that you had moved here? When I think back on it, it seems like it did not take him long to figure out where you had taken the kids. I remember you telling me you had told your friend, Reenie, and he must have found out from her. But why would she give him your address?"

Stunned by my question she steps back, defiant. "Why are you asking about how he found us? If you must know, I wrote and told him how good it is here and how the sun always shines for me each morning. He deserved to know where his kids were. I don't answer to you Donna."

Warning bells go off in my head. We've been down this road too many times, we are simply saying and promising things we have said before. I am realizing that I am ignoring boundaries and crossing where I have no right to be. I need to calm down. I try to take deep breaths as I watch her defend her position, shocked that I have put her in this position. I am way out of line. My own emotions are warring with me.

"How can you understand! You have your nerve treating me like this. He is getting counseling, he promised to get a job—any job. You saw how much he helped when the kids and I were sick. He means it this time, Donna; I can tell when he is lying. He really is sorry for what happened.

I must accept some of the blame too. He is like the Lenny I married. I believe him and I am happy to have him back home with us. I did not for one minute believe he would pack up and follow us. When I think back on it, it just shows how much he does love us. He had to leave a job he loved doing, one that paid well. You don't have any right to judge my actions or how I am handling what is happening now. I know him better than anyone and I know he will not break his promises to me this time. I am proud of him. How can you say those things to me! Her lip is trembling, I watch her struggle to remain in charge. "It's not easy to accept responsibility for bad behavior and to admit to past mistakes. If you can't accept this, then I really believe you need to stay away from our home. We can keep our contact limited to down here on the streets. I would miss not seeing you for coffee every now and then and I know my kids love it when you come over. Please, please try and understand how I feel. I love him, you know, and I am sure this time it will all work out." Pleading, Annie reaches out takes my hand in hers.

I am moved by her actions and I squeeze her hand in mine. I am humbled and I feel remorse that I have created this untenable situation. She looks cute but resolute, standing there daring me.

I acquiesce. "OK, Annie. I can see you are happy, and you are right—it really is none of my business. I am disappointed to learn you lied to me about how Len found you. I love you and your children, and I worry a lot that he won't be able to stick to his word. It is a good thing he is in counseling. Good for him! I am and will continue to walk this walk with you. Please be honest with me as time goes on, Annie. If things start to get out of hand, let me know and let Sarah know as well so she can be there for the children. None of us want them to witness any more violence. I'll see you next Thursday. Stay safe out here and call me anytime." I hug her and walk away.

I still can't believe how I let my own emotions lead me. I am horrified I was aggressive. This is where my lack of training shows. I put Annie in a defensive position, forcing her to defend Len even more. I believe Len will not change! What if Annie turns back to drugs and drinking? I have now put Annie in a position where she may wonder if I am truly on her side. Hindsight is always easy even if it hurts and leaves such a lot of guilt in one's heart.

May 9, 2017

It doesn't take long for Annie's life to become tumultuous once again! It is less than a month after we had had our long clash on the streets, right after Len returned home after the last major debacle. My phone rings at about midnight. I am guessing at the time, but it seems right. I know I was sound asleep when it rang, jarring me awake.

"OK, this doesn't look good, what is going on that you are calling me in the middle of the night?" I sleepily ask, knowing who it is, after glancing at call display.

Weeping, Annie begs me to come over right now!

"Can't it wait until morning Annie; it is the middle of the night and I was fast asleep."

She is wailing. "It's urgent something terrible has happened."

Now I am scared believing she has maimed or even killed Len. I wish Gipp was here so he could come with me, but he is in Vancouver doing voiceovers.

I drive over to Annie's and when I arrive and enter the apartment, Annie is sitting at the kitchen table crying. Len is sitting across from her, his arms dangling between his legs and his head down.

"I am very relieved to see Len is okay and nothing is amiss. I wonder though, what could be so terrible they need me tonight. The apartment is neat and tidy. "What is so urgent that couldn't wait until the morning?" I pull out a chair and sit beside Annie.

They both start talking at once.

"Slow down, one at a time please. Where are your children?"

"They are sleeping." they echo.

"I didn't mean for anyone to get into them," Len moans.

Annie seems high, still coherent enough to tell me what happened. She stands and begins and paces back and forth, staggering slightly.

She starts to whine and explain, her hands are in motion as she speaks rapidly.

"I knew I was too weak if I ever had access. I begged him so many times not to bring his drugs home where I or the kids could find them," Annie turns to give Len an attempt at an evil eye, but she seems to have trouble focusing on him. "I was putting away some clothes in his drawers and found the coke. I just took a smidgeon on my finger and licked it. It felt so good I snorted more. I'm so sorry Lenny, I know I should not have gone into your drawers, even to put away your socks and underwear. I always leave them on the bed so as not to put my nose where it doesn't belong. I think I knew what I would find if I moved things around and sure enough, I did. I promise I won't do it again, but please don't bring any more here

Lenny, please! It is too much of a temptation for me. I am only a couple of months into my sobriety." Her attempts to be firm are lost in the haze she seems to be in.

She sits again and wrings her hands. She is slipping away from us and struggles not to nod off. Her eyes droop and she jerks her head up trying to keep focused.

I know this situation is a lot worse than either of them, understand. It told me that Annie was not going to be strong enough to stay sober. The least little blip in her life is going to send her into a tailspin and she is going to reach for something to get her through it. My stomach is churning, and I feel nauseous just thinking about the consequences. I am having doubts that I am qualified to even begin to try and sort through all the ramifications of what is taking place here tonight. I try to think of what to say, reminding myself on how our last encounter like this turned out. She has faith in me, but I am not convinced she has the inner strength to ward off her cravings. I believe she probably went looking for drugs, knowing that Len had likely stashed some somewhere in the apartment. Heroin is so easy to get on the streets and cocaine is readily available and the drug of choice for many people. Chrystal meth is cheap and is everywhere, opiates are prolific on the streets. My heart is racing, praying Annie doesn't search them out.

I take a deep breath and pray I can do this in a way that won't get either of them on the defensive. "Let's talk this through," I say. "Len, you can't take the blame for Annie going into your drawers and seeking out drugs. You though know how risky it is for you to even have them in this apartment. Not just for Annie, but for your children as well. Hindsight is great but it is best for Annie and your children for you to get any and everything out of here, including any liquor you have. I'm not qualified to advise you on what to do about your own addictions other than to seek help in getting clean and sober.

Annie, you need to get to a counselor tomorrow and get advice on what to do now. You know that you have jeopardized your sobriety and now you are very vulnerable to your addictions. If you don't get the help you need, you are going down that rabbit hole again. I am not qualified to help you in this, I will walk with you as you go through it again, but you need to get on top of it right away. Whatever I can do to help I will. There is nothing more we can do here tonight. You both handled it well and you know what you need to do to ensure everyone is protected. I trust you will get all of the drugs and liquor out first thing tomorrow. This could have waited till morning, I appreciate your trust in me but, please try and think it through the next time you reach for the phone to call me in the middle of the night. In the meantime, I am going home to get some sleep and I will wait to hear from you in the morning. I advise you to seek Sarah out tomorrow, to see if she can take your children for a few hours so you can take care of everything. I'm truly sorry this has happened, but you can both do something positive to end it right now. Take good care and good night." I left to go home.

* * *

The next day, I wander in my garden drinking a cup of tea and I have a million thoughts running through my head. All focusing on Annie and her family.

I have a sinking feeling in my heart. I keep seeing her high on coke and trying to make excuses for why she had taken it and at the same time blaming Len for bringing it into her home. I sincerely hope this is only a slip and that Annie won't use again, but deep in my heart and the knowledge I have from my fifteen years of dealing with these situations, is that disaster is just around the corner.

I look around my garden and green lawn and at my wonderful neighbors and compare my life and Annie's. I live in a lovely middle-class neighborhood, where children have lots of yard to run around in and many have pets, they care for. They often burst outside and yell and carry on like a bunch of rabid animals, dashing here and there and chasing their dogs or each other in mindless pursuit. Adults gather and enjoy occasional barbecues where we all get together, play guitars, and sing while our children and grandchildren scream and laugh the evening away. None of us are rich monetarily, but we are rich in support, love, and joy. I never have to think about where my next meal is coming from, I don't have to sell myself in order to ensure my family has the bare necessities, nor do I have to worry about being physically abused by my husband. I know the names of all my neighbors on my cul-de-sac. I often stop to chat with whomever is out in their yard weeding. Or if they are chatting with another neighbor, I am comfortable joining in their conversation.

My life, in contrast to Annie's, is safe and comfortable. She is always under stress worrying about finances, her children's needs, and her husband's short fuse. She knows the name of one neighbor only—albeit a wonderful friend. She must pack up her children to take them to a park to run and play safely outside. I know others are worse off than that, but the reality for me is I see the harsh lifestyle Annie is caught up in. No one of us should sit in judgment on another. I walk back into my home, sick at heart and praying that Annie will be able to stay strong, clean, and sober. I know she is on a slippery slope and all I can do is walk beside her and try and give her the hope and strength and enough love to help her make it through this crisis. I pray that the high she felt last night is not seductive enough to pull her into her addiction again.

Neither Annie nor Len have called yet. I pick up my phone and call Annie to see how she is.

"Hi, Annie. How is everything this morning?"

"Oh my gosh, Donna," she says. "I can't remember most of last night. Can you believe I was so stupid to get high again? That's not going to happen ever again. I made Lenny get all the stuff out of here and he promised he would never bring it home again. I even made him promise no booze in the house, either. I know I am strong enough not to fall back on that stuff again, but I don't want it anywhere near my kids. He should know better, don't you agree? He's gone out to his friends where he sometimes stays and he going to stash it all there. His friend uses, too, so Lenny says he won't care but Lenny says he needs to put it where his friend can't find it and steal it.

That's the reason he brought it here. He told me his friend got into his stash and stole all of it and used it himself. He was good about removing it from here. I love how he has changed so much when he comes home. He helps with the housework and he is an amazing dad. My life is ultra-right now. I am sorry I took part of his stash here and used it; that will never happen again." She was almost babbling she talked so fast and often repeated things, which made me wonder if she might still be a bit high.

"I'm happy to hear that, Annie. You know how easy it is to fall off the wagon and start using again. That high is so elusive. We both know you will keep running after it as you need more and more to feel that good, it is that seductive, I'm proud of you and know you will do everything in your power not to be pulled into that lifestyle again. Just keep a picture of those two adorable children in your mind and you will find the courage to fight against it.

Please phone your counselor this morning and make an appointment to see her. Be sure you tell her about last night. Be totally honest with her, Annie. Let her know that you searched for the drugs and that Len did nothing to entice you, other than keeping them where you could find them. Please let me know how all that goes when I see you later this week. I need to get going as I have a hair appointment. Take good care, Annie, and I will see you Thursday night. Call me if you need me and go carefully, my friend. I keep you in my heart and prayers always."

June 22, 2017

My days seem to disappear without me noticing until Thursday is upon me. As usual, I still haven't prepared my little bags or written this week's message on the pass-it-on cards. One of these weeks I will be organized and ready to go long before I need to put dinner on the table for Gipp and me.

As I am walking around the streets that Thursday night, I watch Annie from a distance and notice how thin she is getting. She looks wan and weary. I stop and talk to Misty and then go on over to Annie. Tonight, she has on a sleeveless tan-coloured shirt and white shorts. A pale, yellow sweater is tied to the straps of her small handbag. She has on cute white flip-flops that sport a yellow flower on the top. Her hair is short, and the curls seem to dance around her face as I watch her chat with Jan, another sex trade worker, and laugh over something said.

"You OK, Annie?" I ask as I hand her a gift bag.

"Yeah, I'm pretty good, Donna. Things are getting me down at home. Lenny still has no job, and he is hard to live with these days. The kids seem to be getting to him, which is unusual. As you know, he is patient with them but lately he is on edge most of the time. I don't know how best to handle my life right now. At times I would like for him to get out and find his own place and then I know he would be forced to find a job. I know he is under a lot of pressure and I try to see his perspective on things." She seems deflated and smiles with little warmth.

Trying to keep a positive façade I respond. "I don't know what to say, Annie. You know I believe you should tell him to leave. That would take so much pressure off you. He has no reason to change things if you continue to make excuses for him. I believe he cares more about his drug and alcohol buddies and his own addictions than he cares about you or his children, otherwise he would take any work just to help you out."

I know as soon as those words are out of my mouth it is a mistake. I am right, Annie immediately turns away from me and starts her diatribe.

Her words are clipped, arms are crossed around her chest. "I know how you feel about Lenny, Donna. You will never be able to see his side of this! You just can't believe I know him better than you and I understand what is going on with him. I love him, his children love him, he deserves our support! I'm sorry I said anything to you about what's going on, I had hoped you would be on our side and could offer up some real help instead of the same old prattle. You should leave now. I love the bags you give out and I hope you will continue to stop by and chat with me, but if you are going to go on about how lazy and useless Lenny is, then just don't bother!"

She turns and her eyes are boring through me. Her stance is combative.

I tread lightly here, and my stance is contrite, but my response is dramatic and firm. "I'm sorry, Annie. I am only telling you what I believe. I am on your side. I promise in future I will not bring up anything to do with your home life again unless you ask for my advice. I'll see you next Thursday, unless you need me before then. Again, you can always call me no matter the time. Good night Annie. Stay safe out here. Give your children a hug for me and say hi to Sarah."

"I'll do that, Donna. Good night." She snips.

I have stopped and talked with most of the women. Feeling dejected and sad I turn and walk away. I drive home and am surprised when I walk in to see it is past 1 a.m. I slip into bed and have a restless sleep.

The next morning, I keep to myself. Gipp is busy writing ramblings for his Christmas show and will be gone most of today and tomorrow doing the voiceovers for them. I try to do some writing myself. I love to write poetry, particularly when I feel depressed as I do today, thinking about Annie and our conversation last night.

I remember when I was going to some shelters for abused women, asking a group of them what was the most difficult of their journey once they had made the decision to leave their abusive husbands and take their children to these safe havens. There were several reasons; it was difficult for them to talk about it as it was such a long and tortuous road they traveled before they had the courage to leave.

They talked about how lonely they felt and scared for their safety, but how much more they were afraid to be alone without the financial support of their spouses. They were frightened about what their friends would think and their immediate family members who did not know what was taking place behind closed doors. Their loss of community was a major hurdle.

Some had seen earlier signs of aggressiveness but thought their love for their husbands would change that.

I believe the continual rhetoric their husbands would tell them, words like 'If YOU would stop etc., using relentless words causing the women to feel unworthy. Until they were ultimately convinced, they deserved the bullying tactics used by their mates. They believed what their husbands told them after the abuse had happened—some of the men were contrite and felt terrible about the abuse, they would be sincere in their promise that it would not happen again.'

I begin to see why Annie had become so defensive last night. I understand how easy it is for someone like me, who stands on the outside looking in, finds it so difficult to believe that Annie cannot see how abusive Lenny is. It boils down to his need to control her. Ultimately his control and power convince her that it is not his fault—she has pushed him too far— if only she would stop and think what she is saying or doing that inflames him, none of the abuse would happen. Annie is brainwashed. I realize that I need to butt out, simply support her on the streets. Step in when I am asked to step in unless, of course, he beats her up again. Then I will do everything in my power to get her to kick him out of her life. Annie has been told by the police that they are there to help and protect her. We did call them once, but Annie refused to lay charges. The attending officer did everything he could do to convince her to let him talk to Len, but she was having none of it. She remained adamant. Each time we tried to get the police involved she refused and told us she would deny anything if we called and told them what was happening. Gipp, Sarah and I, tried and tried to convince her that not only would the police do everything they could to help but the authorities would have a record of the abuses. It was to no avail. She refused to act on our pleas. I told her about the organizations that help abused women. How they provide shelter for them and their children and find them housing and support once they are strong enough to function on their own.

I know I am not a qualified counselor. I am sorry to learn she has quit going to the one we had set up for her. My friend, the counselor we had set up for her had called me to tell me Annie had quit going to her. She asked me to speak with Annie to try to get her to go back for counseling. I tried but Annie reiterated she could look after herself and did not need anyone telling her how she should live her life. I feel blessed to have the contact I have with Annie and her adorable children. I pray that doesn't end. I can't pretend to know the answers.

Annie

I wonder, too, how different Len seems to be when I talk with him, how often he seems baffled by my accusations. This puzzles me.

August 17, 2017

Time moves along and I watch Annie steadily go downhill each week. She is using again and losing weight. She is withdrawn when we talk. I try to encourage her to go back to counseling and get the help she needs. I can see she is too sad and alone for me to reach her. I check on her children by calling Sarah and learn that Len takes them out most days while Annie tries to sleep. Sarah tells me there are loud verbal fights and when they get too volatile, she slips over and takes their children out. Or, if it is at night, often the children slip out on their own and go to her place. Both Sarah and I are concerned for Annie and the children, but if she doesn't ask for help, we cannot do more than offer it. I know there is no point in calling in the authorities or organizations, who are there to help. Annie has threatened to tell anyone I call on her behalf that she would tell them I stalk and berate her. Len is on site and ensures the children are safe. He has assured Gipp the times Gipp has gone to take the children to the playground that he is watching out for them. After watching how tender and caring Len is with his children and how his attitude toward me has changed, I don't feel threatened by him.

I know it is just a matter of time before it all comes tumbling down. Sure enough, I get a call one night from Annie, begging me to come over. When I arrive, she is a mess, she is high, has a black eye, and the children are wailing. The apartment is strewn with Annie's clothes where she has dropped them where she took them off. I don't know if Len was here when she came home or what. Dishes are in the sink and it all looks depressing as hell. Len is threatening to take the children and leave once and for all. Annie is begging me to do something, but I cannot do anything other than to try and persuade Len to just go, so we can try and sort through it all in the morning. This time, he is having none of it. He has packed up some belongings for the children and gathers them up and leaves.

Annie is wailing and carrying on, screaming, "He can't do this! They are my children and I have been taking care of them all their lives, I have custody, and no one can take them away from me!"

Oh, my Lord, this is a nightmare, she is too high to deal with this or listen to reason. I am sad for her. I see a woman completely out of touch with reality and I know in my heart she will lose her children. I assume he is taking them to a motel. I sit next to Annie, gather her in my arms, and try to console her. After she settles down, I make a cup of tea for us and ask her where Sarah is.

She is a mess, her curls are waging a battle on her head, some are snarled, some droop and are squished together. She has a stain on her black t-shirt and her shorts look like they have never seen an iron. This is not like Annie. Slurring she droops and responds. "She and her family have gone on a holiday and won't be back for a couple of weeks. We need to go and get my kids *right now*, Donna. He has no right to take them from me." She stands and starts to pace unsteadily.

"They are safe for tonight, Annie. I don't know where Len took them, do you?"

She frowns and looks at me in disbelief. "How would I know? He never tells me anything. He punched me in the face like the bully he is. No one is going to give my kids to him. I'm their mother—they belong with me!" she is trying hard to stand firm.

She needs sleep, I gather her to me and speak softly. "Let's get you into bed now, Annie. You are in no condition to do anything right now. We don't know where Len took your children, so you are better to get some rest and you will be able to see everything more clearly in the morning. I am sure Len will be over with the children then, and you can both work through this and come up with something that works."

I walk her to her bedroom, and she falls face down on the bed. She is out of it and passes out almost as soon as she hits the bed. I remove her sandals and cover her with a blanket and wait awhile to ensure she remains asleep. I will call in the morning and pray that Len brings the children home early tomorrow.

I have a feeling of dread that this is the end for Annie. I am convinced that Len will get custody and Annie will continue this downward spiral. I can't do any more tonight, so I go home and get little sleep myself.

Annie calls me early in the morning and tells me she doesn't remember anything about what happened last night. She asks about the children and I tell her not to be concerned as Len has them and they are safe. I tell her that I will come over in an hour and, hopefully, Len will have come home with the children by then. We can deal with everything once he arrives. I suggest she take a shower and get dressed. And maybe if she is up to it, she could clean up the kitchen and make things presentable for when they come home. I am uncertain if Len will even bring them back today. I get cleaned up myself then, go over to Annie's.

Len and the children are there when I arrive, and he and Annie are shouting at one another. I let myself in, the door is slightly ajar. I assume Len didn't close it tight. I gather the children and take them to their room. I give them crayons and a colouring book and ask them to colour a picture for me. They look at me with tears in their eyes and ask if mommy and daddy are going to hurt each other.

I hug them to me and inhale their sweetness, they smell like soap. They both nestle my neck with their warm soft faces. "No, they are just upset right now, and I am going to see if I can help them feel better. I would love a picture I can put on my fridge. My children are grown now, I have lots of room for a drawing, and I miss seeing one there." They both smile and say they will each do one. I thank them and go to Len and Annie, who are still carping at one another.

"OK, both of you stop, right now. You are upsetting your children and this yelling is not solving anything. It's time you both come up with a solution that will work well for your children and stop worrying about your own needs and wants." I try to hold my own temper, not too successfully.

"Lenny says that he is taking the kids and they are not coming back here until I clean up my act. He has no right to tell me what I can and can't do. I have custody of my kids and he is not taking them anywhere as long as I am standing." Annie is shaking with rage and fear.

He gets in her face and in a firm, quiet voice sneers. "You are not fit to look after yourself, let alone our children, I am taking them; I have contacted children's services and they are sending a worker over here this morning. They should be here any minute." He plops on a chair.

"Annie is bewildered and fires questions at him. What are you talking about, Lenny? What have you done? I need my kids—you have no right to do this. Who has fed and clothed them the past two years while you have mooched off me, you never help with the rent. She shudders when she stops to take a breath. Her fear of losing her children is palpable. "You hit me and cause nothing but trouble here? You need to move out and stay out of our lives until you get a job. How can you look after them? You don't even have a place to live or a job to buy food and stuff. You will never get custody; I am a good mother. I am not addicted to anything; I can easily get off drugs. This is my apartment, my furniture, my kids. Get out now!" she screams, shoving him.

"I'm not going anywhere until the person from children's services gets here," he replies, again arrogantly.

I am frightened he is going to hit her. He doesn't, he moves away from her. I am at a loss; I try to sort through what is happening and I stammer. "OK, both of you sit down. I'll make some coffee. Do you have cream in the fridge, Annie?"

She seems frozen in time, and dumbfounded. "Yes, I just shopped a couple of days ago." She stiffly sits at the table.

Len glares at her. I put on the coffee pot and there's a sudden knock on the door. The noise makes me jump; I am that nervous.

Annie gets up and opens the door, inviting the lady from children's services in.

I am filled with dread. I fear Annie is going to lose custody. She is still dazed and seems to be in shock. I am petrified she is going to lose control. Len, on the other hand, is quiet and seems well-prepared to deal with whatever is ahead. Both children come running out when they hear the knock on the door. I gather them to me and take them back into their room and ask them to do another picture for me. I quietly leave the room and get a cup of coffee, then go back to them. Later, what feels like an eternity, I hear the woman leave.

I creep out of the room with the children in tow. "What's happening?" I ask Len. I see Annie, hands covering her face, mumbling "No, no, no."

"I'm taking the kids with me for two months. Annie has that long to get clean and sober in detox. At that time, they'll reassess the situation and advise if they will be returned here to her. I'm sorry, Donna, but she is too unpredictable. And as long as she is using drugs, the children will stay with me," Len says, going to the children's bedroom, where he packs some of the children's things, grabs his jacket and their coats and leaves with them. Saying nothing more he quietly shuts the door. "Are we going to the park, daddy?" I hear the children excitedly ask Len.

I am baffled that children's services could conclude and decide to give Len custody, just like that, with so little evidence and I wondered why this woman had come out so quickly and made that snap decision. I understand that Annie is in no condition to deal coherently, but that is likely her fear for her children and her inability to rationalize what is taking place. I am totally confused myself. I just wonder if this might be a set-up, where Len has created a scenario with a friend. I am puzzled by all of it.

By now, Annie is crying hysterically, totally out of control. There is no point in my trying to reason with her until I can get her to settle down. I put on the kettle and make some tea. I remove the cup of coffee that hasn't been touched. I search the cupboard for some sugar and notice some cookies. I put some on a plate and take the teapot, cups, and cookies and set them down. and sit down next to

Annie. I gently place my hand on her shoulder, handing her a box of tissues that are set on the table.

"What am I going to do without my kids?" she sobs taking it.

I wait until she has had time to drink her tea and has settled enough to have a coherent discussion on what has transpired. I watch her slowly get control. I hand her a cookie and watch her nibble at it. She seems weary and desolate. She slumps down on her chair and looks like someone who has lost all hope.

I hesitantly start to make suggestions. "This is just temporary, Annie; you need to get back into detox and then you can get custody again."

She responds listlessly. "You know how long the wait list is to get into detox, Donna? She hiccups. It could take months before I get in. It's not fair. I have been looking after them and making sure they have everything they need; she takes great gulps of air trying to speak over her sobs.

"Len has done nothing but bleed me dry and he's the reason I am a basket case all the time. I am scared and worried I won't be able to make the rent or make certain I have enough money to look after everything my kids need. Why can't that woman see that? This is my place; he's renting a motel room. What kind of security is that? We both know he uses, too, and he drinks in front of the kids all of the time! I can stop using anytime I choose. I only take hits to settle my nerves." She is rambling, doing her best to convince me she can care for her children.

I take a drink of tea, trying to think how I can get Annie to accept her situation. "I know it doesn't seem fair right now, Annie, but you will have this time to get off the drugs and you will be able to do some extra things—maybe even plan a little get away for you and your children when you have completed your program. You will be able to save some money each month to enable you to do that. I don't think you have had any time off since you arrived here, have you?"

She looks at me like I have two heads. "God no! All my time and money have gone into our living expenses' Since Len came back. I have had to use my credit card and I owe money on it. I should be able to pay it off over the next couple of months. I can do this Donna—for my kids I can do anything. You saw how good I looked after them when I first got here. You know it was only after Lenny came that things changed, and I changed. I'm going to go cold turkey. I have only been back on heroin for a couple of weeks. I can get off on my own. I'll see if I can go back to seeing my counselor. Will you help me Donna?" She hiccups.

"I have no experience nor any training in how to deal with anyone who is detoxing, Annie. I will be here to support you in any way I can, but I believe you should get professional help. It won't be easy, as you know from your previous experience, and I don't believe it is a good idea to try to do it on your own. I take another drink of tea, letting what I say sink in. I can't be here 24 hours a day and I believe that is what it is going to take for you to beat this. Let's draw up a plan that might work for you. We'll make a list in order of the things you need to do to get started and stay on the program. The first thing you will need to do is get hold of your counselor and advise her what your plans are and get her to go over what we have written down and see if she agrees. Once we have completed your list, I think for the rest of today you should get some rest and start on this journey tomorrow. I put my arm around her, my heart aches seeing her downtrodden expression. I swallow my own sorrow and go on to say.

Remember, Annie, you can't give up, because if you do, you may not get your children back. You and Len are now on their radar and children's services will keep a tight rein on you. You have a tough road ahead for the next month, but you know in your heart that you have no choice. Your love for your children must be first and foremost ahead of your desire for drugs. The ball is in your court, Annie. No one else can do what needs to be done. Let's get started on that list," I ramble on, smothering the urge to cry. I can feel her anguish.

It takes us two hours to get the list completed in the order we believe will work best. I just hope and pray she can do it. She looks crushed and hopeless. I am frightened to my core that what's ahead is going to be too difficult.

"OK, Annie, we have done all we can do today. I'm going home. I am at the end of the phone, but please try and get some sleep. Don't go out tonight—stay home and watch TV or read a book. I'll see you tomorrow night on the streets if you don't need me during the day. Take good care and know I am praying for you and I love you." I walk out the door and feel terrible leaving her alone. I have been gone for several hours; I am sure Gipp will be getting antsy. He is home and I want to be with him. I feel totally exhausted.

I can't understand how Len could get custody and all of a sudden has enough money to rent a motel and care for their children. Or how he got children's services involved so quickly. He must have had that motel room for a while and was socking away some of his welfare money. How unfair life seems at times.

September 28, 2017

The next month is a disaster! Annie is deeper into drugs and has lost any desire to get off them. No matter what I try to do to help, my words and actions fall on deaf ears. She is too sad and deeply depressed. I have called her counselor, but she says she has tried to get her to come in and even offered to go to Annie's home, but to no avail. Sarah called me a week ago and said that Annie is going to be evicted if she doesn't pay her back rent and this month's rent. Sarah says she can't talk to Annie anymore; she is usually too high or coming down off a high. She told me that Annie has not seen her children or made any effort to see them for more than a week. Annie has given up and Sarah doesn't feel comfortable having her around Jamie. She asks me not to judge her; she has tried every way she can to help, but Annie refuses to hear anything Sarah says.

I called Sarah to assure her that what Annie is doing is her own choice. Until she can get detoxed, she won't be able to do anything and will probably lose custody of her children. Children's services may even take them into care. I told her that I had been over to the motel where Len and the children are living and the conditions aren't great, but the children seemed to be fine. One time, when I went to deliver some food to another woman, who coincidentally was living in the same motel, I saw the children playing and running around with other kids. Len and a couple were sitting and visiting. They seemed to be watching the children. I felt sick to my stomach to see what was happening with the children. I was saddened by the fact the children were losing their mom and I wondered if Len would take good care of them. It is so heartbreaking to watch how children are lost and forgotten when parents get hooked on drugs and lose all perspective. Nothing and no one counts more than that release from reality that the drugs bring, or so the addicted person believes.

After Annie got evicted, I saw her in a homeless shelter, and she seemed to be hooked up with a guy; they were living in a room there. She looked wasted and out of it; I don't know if she even recognized me. It is soul-shattering to watch a sweet, loving mom end up in such a terrible lifestyle. I couldn't give up on her and, when I walked away, I made a promise to myself to go back the next morning and see if she were sober enough to talk to me.

When I got home, I sat down and decided to read a little before I got ready to go to bed. My thoughts kept breaking in, and I kept drifting away, losing focus on the words on the pages. I set the book down. I closed my eyes and thoughts of Annie swirled. I could see Annie when she first arrived here. That first night I saw her, I remember how sweet and pretty she looked. When I approached her on the street that night, she was shy and reserved. She seemed almost nervous and maybe a little frightened of me. I learned that she needed furniture and other things as she had left her home and husband in Prince Albert and had driven here with her two small children. All that mattered to her were her babies and setting up a new home for them.

She quickly met Sarah, who became a very, good friend to her and her children over the couple of years that she lived in the apartment across the hall. I started to weep, remembering how excited and happy she was to be free and able to live her life with no fear. I was amazed at how brave she was to make such a drastic move on her own. She was determined to keep her children safe and happy. She planned to go back to school to get her Grade 12 and from there she would move on to get trained in being a professional photographer. She wanted to take photographs showing the beauty of nature, the city, and outlying areas. She always told me that she loved how the sun never stopped shining here.

She loved living here. She spent those early days, working on her courses and taking her children to parks and lakes and going somewhere new each weekend. She told me it was important for her children to see her getting that high-school diploma and making something of herself. She never intended to stay in the sex trade longer than one year, but fate had a different road for her to travel down.

Annie

The tears were streaming down my face as I remembered this wonderful young mom who wanted to be that role model for her children. I believe she would have made her dreams if life hadn't taken her down a path she wasn't prepared for. I don't believe it was just one thing that went wrong for Annie. I can't help but believe her life would have taken a different turn if she had remained on her own for a couple of years. I believe we just keep making the wrong decisions and they pile up. All the stress she dealt with broke her resolve and she sought escape in drugs. Now, I watch a broken spirit and a lost soul crawl through each day and each night buried in the darkness and aloneness of addiction. I am devastated when I think of her children living with their dad in less than satisfactory conditions or locked in the system with many other children, waiting for someone to love them again. I turn out the lights and go to my bed, my own spirit broken and aching for Annie.

I lay in bed; my thoughts are swimming with ideas on how to get her off the streets and into detox. I know it can't be my idea and that if Annie does not want to get clean and sober, I will have no influence over that. I feel desperate and long for a simple answer, knowing there is none. I thrash around and I want to scream at my helplessness. I pray to my God to "Please, please get into her heart and give her the hope she needs to move forward." Finally, I fall asleep, worn out with despair for my ineptness and hope in my God and the strength that I know is buried in Annie's heart. I can do no more than love her and walk with her, always leading her toward release from the devil lodged in the drugs she releases into her system.

September 29, 2017

I wake up feeling as weary as I did when I crawled into my bed last night. I promise myself I will go down to the homeless shelter and try to find Annie and take her to a restaurant and buy her a decent breakfast. Hopefully, she will be coherent enough to listen to the proposal in my head, which I have now written down in point form to make it easier to understand. I know she may not even want to go anywhere with me. She may be too high to even be able to put any coherent thoughts together. I believe that, at this point, I am more desperate than Annie is. I tell Gipp that I am going down to see if I can find Annie and that I will be back either very quickly or not for a couple of hours or more. He is OK with that as he has a full day of recording his Christmas shows. I kiss him goodbye and head out.

I drive to the shelter I found Annie in last night and learn that people must leave early in the morning and return later in the day for refuge. I see tents still up across the road and start asking at each one if Annie is there.

She isn't. I head over to another area where I know she sometimes hangs out and find her there. Annie seems forlorn but is hungry and agrees to come with me to get some breakfast.

"Thank you for giving me some of your time Annie. How are you doing? Can I help you in any way?"

I know my questions are mindless, but I am barely hanging on seeing Annie in the condition she is in. She is rail thin, pale, and haggard. Her hair is long, the curls are limp and loose. Every bit of her requires attention. She is wearing a baggy, gray, sweat-shirt and loose-fitting black pants. Her boots are scuffed but don't look worn. She looks lost and I watch her struggle to force the food down. I can see she is starving, but she is dope sick and I wonder if she will throw up later. I can't express the hatred I have for the drugs that are so accessible on our streets. The damage they do is endless. I understand how desperate Annie's body is for food, but I know her focus is to get a fix today.

She wearily looks at me and asks. "I'm OK, Donna. Have you seen my kids? Are they OK? Is their daddy looking after them? I miss them so much. Maybe I could get to see them today? Do you think you could help me to see them, Donna? Please? I will clean up and be steady once I finish eating. I need to see them. I miss them, I want to tell them I love them, and I will be getting them back as soon as I can find an apartment and get back to my work." She pleads with me and starts to weep; the tears flood her face.

I reach out and take her hand in mine.

I tamp down my sorrow and tell her. "I can't do that Annie; I don't know where Len lives. I haven't seen him in months. I am sure your children are fine and being looked after. You know that children's services will keep them safe if Len doesn't. You need to look after yourself, Annie, and get into a program that will help you to get off the drugs and back to being able to look after them again. I know they know how much you love them; they are always going to remember that. Let me help you get into detox and find a safe place to live once you are clean and sober. I love you Annie and I know you can do that. I have watched you come through some harsh stuff and I know how strong you can be. Please say you will let me help you." I hope I don't sound as desperate as I feel.

She sighs and does her best to perk up. "Do you think we could drive around and maybe see if we can find Lenny and the kids? We could spend some time at the park with them. Can we do that now, Donna? I have had enough to eat. I feel really good now."

I don't have the heart to tell her that one of the other working women had told me she had heard Len no longer has custody of their children. She went on to tell me he had lost custody before but told my friend he was going to get them back. I know it will break Annie's heart to know they are probably in the system and that children's services now has custody.

"We can't do that until you get into detox and find a place to live that is suitable for them. They can't live with you if you are using drugs. You can barely look after your own needs right now. Let's drive over to the emergency ward at Victoria General Hospital and see if we can get some help for you today. The longer you put it off, the harder it is to get the help you need. You cannot do this on your own, Annie. Please come with me."

I stand up and reach for her hand. She pulls away.

Her demeanor changes in a heartbeat, she angrily says. "Why can't you drive me around to find my kids? I don't need to go to detox; I can clean up myself. I want to hug my kids and tell them I love them. I want to take them to the park and play with them. I don't want to do anything else. If you cared as much as you say you do, you would drive me around and let me spend some time with them. You're no different than any of those other do-gooders who always try to get us to go to detox or the psych ward. I can get clean and sober any time I want. I don't need anyone else to help. Go on. Leave me alone. I'll walk around and find them myself. Thanks for the food. I'll see you around." She staggers out of the restaurant.

I certainly did not handle that right. I don't know that I can do anything more than just keep tabs on her. She still has my number and has called me several times over the past few months when she has needed someone to talk to. It is always the same conversation. She wants to see her children, to hold them, and tell them she loves them. She is sure she can kick her addiction anytime she wants to. It just isn't the right time yet, or it is my fault for not helping her to find her children. This is the one light in her life I cling to. As long as she still carries the love of her children in her heart, to the point where she desires to see them, it gives me hope. I know she is not totally lost to the drugs yet—that yearning will keep her on the edge of freedom.

I once again lift her up in prayer to my God. I hope with all my heart that this will all seem like a nightmare one day. A nightmare I can share with her when she is clean and sober. Until then, I will continue with my street ministry and always be there when she calls.

October 30, 2017

About a month later, I get a call from Annie, asking me to meet her at the hospital. When I arrive, I see her standing outside with a plastic bag containing her belongings. She has some clean clothes on and looks like her old self, except she is bone thin and still pale as a ghost and she has a tummy bump that is impossible to miss.

"Hi, Annie. Are you OK? You look a lot better than the last time I saw you." Such a lame greeting but I couldn't think of anything else to say. I feel sad to see her standing there alone with a forlorn, lost expression.

"Yeah, I just went through a bad spot, but I'm OK now. Thanks for coming to get me."

"No worries, I'm not doing anything that can't wait. Have you had breakfast? We can go and have something, or just go for coffee. Whatever suits you."

"Yeah, I'd like that. I could use some decent food after eating hospital food for a couple of weeks."

"Yeah, we can all relate. I would like something sweet. There's a small restaurant across the street; we can go there if that's OK with you. Climb in and we'll drive over."

"OK."

We get a table and order our food and coffee.

"So, Annie. What can I do to help you?"

"Not much. I'm pregnant. My boyfriend says he'll look after me. He lives in a shelter and has a room." She talks as she reaches for her coffee.

"Wow! That's exciting. Are you both happy about the baby?" I ask, not knowing what else to say.

"Yeah, we are getting some help. I have a worker who will set up with an organization who helps women like me. They give baby clothes and furniture and all kinds of help. I'm really excited."

"That's great, Annie. When are you due? What's the dad's name? Is he able to get a job to help you?"

"Yeah, he works part-time now. I am five months along, so not too long to wait. My boyfriend's name is Roger. He's super nice; you'll like him. Maybe we could come over for coffee sometime and you could get to know him. He's going to go to detox as soon as he gets some money together, so we can get groceries and stuff. We figure by the time the baby comes along, we will be all ready and waiting for him or her." She smiles as she takes a spoonful of food.

"It sounds as if you are happy and pretty settled." In my mind I am not convinced. The fact that Roger is still using is a red flag and I worry that Annie may succumb and become addicted again. She is just out of the hospital and is going right back into that lifestyle again, only now she is carrying a baby. I worry for the baby because she has been using drugs all along up until a month ago. I am filled with dread, even as I try to share her joy.

"Yeah, it's going to be good. Have you seen Len and my kids lately," she asks?

I know I have no option but to let her know what I have heard and brace for her reaction.

"No, Annie. The last I heard was that Len has not had custody of your children for several months. I was told they are under the care of children's services and in foster care right now. I heard they are living in a home near Oak Bay. I don't know where but was assured they are being well looked after. I'm not sure of anything else. I don't know what school they go to, either. This is just what I have heard; I do not know any of this for a fact. When I last saw Len, he was clean and sober, but I have not seen him for quite a long while."

"Oh my God! How could Len let that happen? I need to get custody of them right now. How do I get them back? Tell me what I have to do." She shoves her plate away and pleads with me to help.

Damn I wish I had not said anything, just let on I didn't have any information. I hesitantly respond. "You would have to go to children's services and prove that you are in a position to provide for their care. You will need an apartment and furnishings and all the things a family needs to survive. You might be able to find out where they are and maybe even visit with them. I don't know how the system works. You are their mother and I'm pretty sure you have some rights. What they are or what you will be required to do are things I know nothing about."

I ramble on, wishing I were anywhere but here. "How do you think Roger will react once he knows you want to bring them into your relationship? Annie, you know this is old information and I don't know how accurate it is, Len may have custody again by now, we just don't know." I try to sound hopeful, but I truly have no idea where they are or what her chances are of seeing them.

She nonchalantly chatters on. "Oh, he will be OK with it. He told me he loves children; he doesn't have any of his own, but soon he will. We never talked about mine. I guess I was too involved to get around to introducing him to them. To be honest, I never knew where they were. I thought they were with Len. I often thought maybe he took them back to Prince Albert, where our families could help. She picks up her fork like she is going to start eating again but she leans her elbow on the table still holding the fork in the air, begins to speak again. "I never thought he would give them up. I'm really sorry about that. I wish I could hold them and tell them how much I love them and will never stop loving them. Will you help me get in touch with children's services and see if I can see them? Tell them I have a room and a man who is helping and that we are going to have a baby. They'll have to give them back to me once they see I am clean and sober and have a place for them that's safe." She sounds excited but I am doubtful she will get custody yet. It would be wonderful if all of what she says were realistic. I look at her and wonder if she is strong enough to face the journey ahead of her.

I smile wanly "I will get the information you will need to contact them. I will be happy to go with you when they set up an interview, where they will evaluate you and Roger and your living conditions to ensure you are able to provide all that your children need."

She immediately goes into combat mode. "What do you mean 'evaluate' us? I am their mother, they belong to me, and I want them back now. No one can love them as much me, and I know Roger will love them too. We're not rich, but we can give them what they need. I looked after them by myself when I came here. You know that, and you can vouch for me. You can tell them what a good mother I am. You'll do that won't you?" she says, swiping at her leaking tears.

I dial back a bit. "I can only tell them what I know, Annie. I am not an expert. Yes, I know you can be an excellent mom and your children love you, but you have had some serious issues in the past. You must know your drug use was the deciding factor in your losing custody in the first place. If Roger is using drugs, you know they will not give you custody. Are you sure you can stay off them if they are in your home? It is all going to be looked at and if in fact they are in their custody, I doubt they will relinquish custody to you until you have proven you can stay off drugs. You will need a bigger apartment and proof that you or Roger can support them." I take a breath hoping she won't go ballistic on me.

"I would start just by seeing if you can visit with your children and maybe spend time alone with them at a park or playground. See how they interact with Roger and he with them. Give them some time to adjust. Think what a devastating blow it would be for them if you got custody too soon and had to give them up again for whatever reasons. You need to think of what is best for them." I am trying to be as gentle as I can with my words. I don't want Annie hurt, anymore either, but the children's welfare is what is most important.

"There is no point getting all upset until we know for sure where they are. I'll get the phone number and you can call and ask the caseworker who answers if they are under their care. Let's go back to my place and see if you can get that information today." We walk to my car and drive to my place. I call give Annie the number for Children's Services and she calls.

Once Annie is connected, with an agent, she is told they can't give her any information over the phone and that she should arrange an appointment to go in and speak with them in person. When they have confirmed that the children are in their care and that she is the mother, they will arrange a visit, provided the foster mom feels it is in the children's best interest.

Anne is visibly upset when she gets off the phone.

"How can they be so mean? They are my babies. I should be able to bring them home now, today!" she complains.

"Come on, Annie. Think about what you are saying. The children are in a safe place being cared for. You must be honest about this; you have not been well enough to care for them for quite a while. You need to follow children's services' instructions and provide all the information they need to arrange a visit. This is good news Annie; you now know where your children are and know you will be allowed to visit them. Who knows, maybe you will eventually be able to provide for them and get custody. You know your children know you love them. This is the best way to show them how deeply you care and are willing to put your children's needs ahead of yours."

I hold her in my arms as she weeps for her children. I hope she understands this is the only option she has.

"Oh, Donna," she moans. "I want so much to hold them and tell them I love them, and I will get them back!"

"I know, Annie, I know." I soothe her as best I can. I feel her agony and my heart wrenches.

November 4, 2017

Sadly, the following days do not go as well as we had hoped. Children's services are busy, and Annie must wait a week to get an appointment with the worker responsible for the care of her children. She is overwrought and is not handling the wait well. I have met Roger and spent a few hours with them both. I am not convinced their relationship will last. I am certain there is no way Annie's children will be turned over to her if they are living in this tiny place.

Roger is an addict and gets little or no work. At this point, he is incapable of getting anything permanent if he continues to use drugs every day. Annie appears to abstain, but I am not certain as I am not here 24 hours a day, nor do I see her every day. I talk to her by phone most days and there have been instances where I thought I heard her slurring her words, but I am not certain. She always promises me that she has not touched any drugs since her release from the hospital, but I know how well an addict can lie about it, so I just keep praying she is protecting her baby and staying off any drug use.

The day of our appointment with children's services starts off well. I pick her up four hours prior to it. I assume Annie will be anxious about her meeting with children's services. I plan to take her to the park and walk around enjoying the fresh air and lovely scenery. I believe she will feel more settled if we have time to be together before. She may have some questions, this way we will have lots of time to get them out of the way beforehand.

"Hi, Annie," I greet her when she gets in my car. "Exciting day. Are you nervous?" I ask, waiting for her to fasten in and get settled.

"A little, but I believe I will get to see them today. After all, I am their mother. They have no right to keep my children from me. I've waited all week for today and they know that."

She seems agitated, and I do not believe she will gain custody at this point. I don't even know if they will let her visit with them or let her take them out to parks or playgrounds.

"Let's not assume anything Annie. Let's take this time to go to Beacon Hill Park and walk and look at the beautiful scenery. I have brought some seeds we can feed to the ducks. I don't know if there will be any animals in the petting zoo this late in the season. When we get out of your meeting let's go and get an ice cream cone."

I am doing my best to relax her and myself. I feel a little anxious too.

She chuckles and answers. "That sound like fun. Let's do it. Roger wasn't home when I called after my doctor's appointment. He is probably out looking for more work. He is excited about this baby and I know he'll man up and look after us. I know he'll love my kids, too. I can hardly wait for them to meet him. You, too, Donna. I know you'll love him. He is kind and loves to be outside as much as I do. He loves walking the trails around the lakes and hiking on the Galloping Goose trail. We've talked about buying bikes so we can ride. I would love to teach my kids to ride a bike and we could go on trail rides as a family. I get excited when I think of all the things we could do together. This beautiful city is my sunshine place; it is always shining here. Let's do it, I'd love to spend the morning at the park and eat ice cream. It sounds so fun," she says as she touches her extended tummy, caressing her baby.

"Let's go. I am happy to see you well again. You look great, Annie!" I tell her as we drive away.

We have a nice couple of hours walking in Beacon Hill Park. We go for a burger and an ice cream cone after we left the park. Annie is anxious for the time to pass so we can go for her appointment. On our way back to my car, she starts to argue with herself the many reasons why they have no right to keep her children from her. Just as we get to where my car is parked. She walks away from me muttering. "We better go now, Annie. We might not find a parking spot close to their office." I call out to her. Still muttering she comes and gets in the car. I can't imagine what she is going through. I'm a mother myself and I am devastated for her. just thinking about me being in her shoes makes my stomach churn.

* * *

"You OK, Annie? I know this is daunting, but I am here to support you. You're a strong woman Annie. Just answer all the questions honestly and let this person see how anxious you are to hold your children and how much you miss them and want them in your life. You haven't taken anything, have you?" I ask hesitantly, afraid she might overreact to my question.

And she does, her back goes up and she turns to me. "Of course not! I keep telling you that I am not using drugs. Don't you believe me? I think I should go to this appointment on my own; you seem determined to convince yourself that I took a hit before you picked me up or maybe you thought I shot up while I took a bathroom break at the park. I don't need you in there with me doubting my every word." She is on a roll, snarling and snipping at me.

I try to calm her down. "Not at all. I am just asking you and, yes, I will keep asking most every time I see you. You must admit, you have not always been honest with me in the past. I am here to back you up and my honor is also on the line here. If I tell them you have been clean and sober since you were discharged, then I need to know that is the truth. If you do not want me to come in with you, that's okay. You seem jittery and I get a sense you are on something, I'm sorry that upsets you Annie. Obviously, I am wrong if you tell me you have not taken anything. I am trying here Annie. I don't want anything to get in the way of you seeing your children. My presence in there isn't going to help you now, I will wait and pick you up after you are done. I have my cell phone with me I noticed you have yours. I drop off Annie for her appointment, praying I am not wrong in that she doesn't need me with her.

"Good! You should know I would never lie to you, Donna," she says as she gets out of my car.

"OK, Annie. I will be in our coffee shop waiting for you to call me to come and get you.

After the interview is over, Annie tells me that Charmaine, the woman from children's services in charge of her children, tells her she believes it is better if Annie waits to see her kids until after the birth of her baby. She believes it will be too disruptive for them and much easier when Annie can meet with them with the baby. She tells Annie that her children are lovely, well-behaved, and are happy where they are. They are together and providing any unforeseen happenings that might change the situation, the family who have them is in for the long haul. That they love her children who have blended in beautifully and are doing well in school. She tells Annie not to worry and promises that she will have the foster parents start to prepare the children for her visit and that she will have a little surprise for them when she arrives.

"I want to see them now. I don't see how it will upset them to see me—I am their mother. I love them, they are mine, and I want them back. I need to see and hold them now. I shouldn't have to wait. It's not fair to them to keep thinking I don't want them," she pleads.

"Annie, I'm going to get us another cup of coffee and then I need you to tell me exactly what she told you?"

She seems guarded. I wonder if she still believes I don't trust her to tell me the truth.

Annie begins to tell me. "No one has ever told them that I don't want them. The children have been told that I am ill and not well enough to care for them right now. They know I am here, and they know I want to have them back. They are well-adjusted and loved in the foster home and she cannot, in fairness to them, disrupt that without preparing them. She doesn't want to give them hope of being back with me. Then if anything goes wrong, and they can't come back to me, it will be devastating for them." She wrings her hands as she continues.

"If things don't work out and the children have to be returned to foster care, there is no guarantee that they would be returned to the same foster family. She said, it is not that long to wait until my baby is born and it gives them time to prepare my children for visits. She told me to be prepared. This is not going to be fast-tracked. It will take several months, possibly even a year before they are ready to remove them from this foster family. It is up to me to convince her I can give them what they need. It is not good enough for me to say I am their mother and I love them therefore I should be given custody. These children came to them damaged emotionally and terrified. She said they have adjusted, and they are deeply loved where they are, and have stability in their lives. She said she was sorry, but my children are her only priority. Please keep in touch with her and she will give me updates on the progress they are making. She had another appoint-ment waiting. She told me to take care of myself and to keep in touch and that I would hear from her shortly. Blah, blah, blah …"

She is getting riled up, running her hands through her hair.

"She can't do that; they are my children. I am the mother and I have rights. We need to get a lawyer and fight her. Who does she think she is? She does not know what is best for my kids. I don't care what the foster parents do or say. They can't love them as much as I do. Just because they have a fancy house and whatever else, does not give them the right to keep my kids away from me. You need to help me get them back, Donna. You know what a good mom I am and why didn't you come in with me? Why didn't you tell that hag that I am a great mom and I love my children more than anyone ever could?" she rails at me.

I try to settle her down by trying to help her make sense of what the woman had told her. "Take a breath Annie. Think about all that she said. It makes perfect sense to do this gradually. She needs to know you can care for your children—loving them is not enough, you must be willing to put them ahead of yourself and Roger. Can you do that, Annie? I didn't come in with you because you never invited me after you told me you didn't want me to come in with you. I thought it was what you wanted. Can you honestly swear that Roger will get a job and support you until you can go back to work once your baby is born? From what you've told me he may have some problems with his own life. Who's going to look after your children while you are in hospital? You don't have someone like Sarah to help you. I work part time and I can't help you. Think about all of this Annie, don't lose hope." I take her hand.

"I know how hard it is for you. I know you can do these things once you put your mind to it, but it will take time. What if he does not want to keep your children once his own child is here? I know you have needs and wants Annie, but what is best for children is what is most important. You gave up any authority when you became an addict and could no longer provide for or care for them. Do what needs to be done to get your children back. I didn't say anything while you explained what she said because I agree with everything Charmaine said.

Glaring, she is ramrod-straight, her mouth is twisted as if she is going to growl, and I am thinking, "If looks could kill ..."

She snarls, "Why do you keep asking questions about Roger, and if I will do everything, they think I should? I have told you of our plans. I know we can do it all, I will do anything to get my kids back. I do not get how she can keep them from me, how can they take kids from their moms and think it is okay. You should be on my side. I am glad you did not come in with me you probably would have smiled and told her she was right. You are supposed to be my friend Donna, be on my side. Why can't you believe what I tell you?"

She has turned her anger on me, staring at me like I'm the reason for all of this. I swear if she had a gun, I believe she might just shoot me. I wish I would learn to keep my mouth buttoned and not believe I have the answers for

Annie. I try to settle her, so she doesn't walk away. I am her ride and I need to know she gets home safely.

"Let's go for a walk, Annie, and stop for another ice cream cone. You'll feel a lot better once you have had some time to think through everything. Try to be happy that your children are happy and being well-cared for. This is a good time for you to prepare for your baby's birth and get things organized so when you do get your visit with your children, it will all come together as it should. Be excited, Annie. You are going to see them and hold them and tell them you will always love them, but for now the best place for them is where they are. Be grateful you do not have to worry that they are not being loved and safe. Come on. Let's go and do some silly stuff and eat junk food, walk on the beach and look for shiny glass pieces. Let's laugh and be free." I do a little twirly dance. She is having none of it.

"I can't, Donna. I don't feel so good. Maybe next week you can call me, and we can do some silly stuff."

"OK, Annie. I'll take you home." We walk to the car. I can get my things together to go down to the streets tonight," I said as I drove her home.

"You all think you're so much better than me. I'll show you all. I will prove I can look after my own kids. I can— wait, you just wait! They are mine and I will fight to get them back," she grumbles as she slams the car door shut and stomps away.

"Phone me if I can do anything to help," I call out to her and then drive away.

February 1, 2018

I keep in touch with Annie and Roger. It is obvious to me that they are both doing drugs. Roger's drug use makes him blatantly oblivious to those around him and he seems like he could care less what anyone thinks. Annie is more subtle, but I know her so well and I can tell when she is high. I try to talk to her about how harmful this is to her unborn baby and how devastating it will be for her when he or she is born addicted and will need to go through detox. How cruel it is for a newborn baby to start life that way.

A couple of weeks later my phone rings, just as I am sitting down for lunch.

I pick up the phone and hear hysterical screaming.

"They are taking my baby from me. You must come! You need to tell them I am a fit and capable mother! You have to come now!" she yells.

"Annie?" I am sure this is her.

She is moaning, obviously upset.

"Yes, my baby was born a week ago, and the lady from children's services told me they are taking my baby away because she is addicted, and I am not capable to look after her while I am addicted to drugs. You know that I am not an addict, Donna. I don't take drugs every day, only when I get depressed and stressed when Roger is too high to work. We need to rely on food banks sometimes, but so do a lot of other moms and they don't take their kids away. I want you to come now. Please Donna, please hurry!"

When I arrive, there is no need for me to enquire where Annie is. I can hear her frantically yelling. I go to where she is, and she runs to me when she sees me.

She is in agony and grief stricken. She falls into my arms, pleading.

"Oh, Donna, please tell them that I am a good mother, and I will take really good care of my baby. They said she is addicted and we both know I did not take enough drugs while I was pregnant to make her an addict. They are lying just because when I went into the hospital, I might have been a little high. I want to take her home now. Everyone knows we all need drugs when we are in labor. They wouldn't even give me any when the pains got really bad!" she wails into my shoulder as I hug her.

My sorrow for her makes my heart ache.

"Try to calm down, Annie. Yelling and screaming is not going to help. There is nothing they can do. They have no alternative but to call in children's services when they are concerned for the baby. They would not tell you she is addicted if she wasn't. Please, come home with me and we'll see what we can do to help you get custody once she has detoxed. "They wouldn't let me take her home with me when she was born. Make them give her to me. Tell them you will look after her." "Annie, she is not here. Someone who knows how to help her through this has her."

She is sobbing uncontrollably. I ease her out of the hospital.

Once we arrive at my home, I finally get her calmed down enough to sit down and have some tea.

"Annie, you must know that you dabbled a little more in drugs than what you thought you had. I know several times I asked you if you were taking any when I came over or when we met for coffee and walks. I believe you did not realize just how often you were high. If you want your baby girl back, you must go back to detox. You cannot live with Roger if he is going to continue to take them. Have you picked a name for her?" I hold her hand while I speak to her. It pains me deeply to see her suffer such pain.

"Hannah." Annie looks at me trying to stop the sob that escapes from her throat. Silent tears fall from her eyes and I start to leak tears too.

"Oh, Annie. This is heartbreaking for you. Have you told Roger yet? Was he with you during the delivery?"

"No, and no, I haven't seen him for a couple of days. I guess he is on a bender. I haven't been able to contact him; he's not answering his cell. I keep trying to reach him, I want him to call me, now Donna!"

"I know Annie, do you have the phone number of a friend who might know?"

"No, he often goes away like this. I never worry because he always comes home." She is weeping and I try to console her.

"Why don't you stay here for a couple of days until you get stronger. We can see what you have to do to meet their requirements to get custody of Hannah." I pour us another cup of tea.

"No thanks, Donna. I need to find Roger and we need to go together to get her back." She gets up and walks unsteadily to the door.

"Annie, you're in no shape to go looking for Roger. You have no idea where he is and at least wait until you contact him on his cell. Stay here and rest; you've had a long arduous day you need to get some sleep. You'll feel a lot better and will be able to think more clearly. Please just stay long enough to sleep a couple of hours."

I take her in my arms and hug her to me. I am deeply troubled, and I ache for her.

"I need to go, Donna; I need to find him. I need to get my baby back now." She walks out the door, shoulders slumped, head down.

I follow her out, I am beside myself. I am afraid for her. I take her hands in mine and plead with her.

"Please do not leave like this, Annie. What difference is a couple of hours going to make? Trust me when I tell you, you will not be able to get Hannah back until she has detoxed and is well and healthy. There is nothing you can do to stop that. What you can do is concentrate on getting into detox and getting yourself strong and healthy again. Whatever you do right now, Annie, please get some rest before you go looking for him. I will drive you back to your place and you can wait for him there. No doubt he will come home soon. Please let me drive you there."

I am desperate and profoundly concerned for her.

"Yeah, OK. But I want to go right now. I want to go home. I promise I'll go to bed and try to get some sleep."

I can see she is worn out and full of anguish, the loss of her baby Hannah is devastating. Her tears leak and she silently brushes them away, too tired to say anymore.

I take her home and am sorry to see they are once again living in a street shelter. I offer to go in with her, but she refuses my offer, telling me she wants to sleep. I drive away, tears pouring down because I know she is too far into her addiction to successfully kick it; she needs to go to detox, but I fear she will simply use the drugs to dull the pain. I pray to my God to give her the strength to do what she will be required to do to get custody of Hannah. It is such a tragic situation for both the baby and the mom. The poor wee baby is forced to go through the agony of withdrawal from her first breath. I try to get angry at Annie and Roger for being so weak and succumbing to their own selfish needs, but I carry too much sorrow for her now.

I try to reach out to her and Roger for weeks after. I go to the shelter several times, but she had left and never returned there. At times I see her at different shelters, once just sitting on the street. But as I approach her, she gets up and walks away. I need to accept that she believes I let her down. I am certain her baby and children were never returned to her. I wonder if she got visiting privileges with her two children. I wonder, too, if Len might have stepped up and gotten custody of them. I assume her baby is put up for adoption or in a permanent foster home. I continue my ministry on the streets, hoping I will see her, but it is to no avail. I never stop looking and I believe that one day I will find her again.

August 23, 2018

It is six months before I see Annie again. It is a Thursday night, and I am at a homeless shelter, when I spot her sitting across the street in front of a blue tent.

"Annie? I ask when I slowly approach her.

"Yeah, whose asking?" she looks up at me with unfocused eyes. I can see she is too high to recognize me. She is unkempt and obviously in need of a bath, and clean clothes.

"It's Donna. I have been looking for you for a very, long time. How are you?" *What a dumb question* I think to myself, knowing in her present state, she probably is unable to put two coherent thoughts together.

"Oh yeah, I remember you," she slurs. She looks right past me, unable to focus.

"I will come back in the morning, Annie. Maybe I could take you for breakfast."

"Yeah, you do that." She is almost asleep.

"Right, then. Good night. I'll be here in the morning before they make you move." I walk away knowing she might not be here tomorrow.

She is there the next morning, but her condition is such that eating breakfast is not on the table. She and a couple of others are packing up and preparing to move to a different location.

"Hi, Annie. Can I drive you somewhere?" I ask.

"I don't know where I am going. Could we come home with you for a few hours till I figure out what to do?" She slurs her words and appears to be wiped out. She is stuck in this miserable lifestyle and I feel helpless.

"You are welcome to come and have a bath and get some fresh clothes. I am sure I have something that will fit you. You are a little taller than me but not by much. You can certainly rest and stay awhile if you like, but I can't have your friends join us."

My offer is made with some trepidation, but she was rail thin and looks done in and she needs a bath and some clean clothes. I am desperate to enfold her in my arms, but I know I cannot. This situation is untenable, and it is entirely up to Annie to decide. She is kneeling on the ground her back is to me as she tosses things into a black plastic bag.

She weaves as she stands to face me.

"These are my friends. Why can't we all come? Are you afraid we will steal from you, or are we not good enough to come with you? I won't know where they are staying, if I come and they find a new place to hang. Do you guys know where we are going?" she asks a guy standing next to her.

"We'll probably head over to John Street and crash down at the shelter, I guess. You should stay with us," he responds. He too looks worn out and is need of a bath, and clean clothes. He has a nice face and smiles as he gently places his arm around her.

"Yeah, I think so, too. Thanks for the offer, Donna. Maybe we can hook up together another time. I'm doing OK. Me and my friends stick together good and no one bothers us too much," she says.

She moves away from her friend and kneels again gathering her belongings.

"OK, Annie. I'll come down later tonight with some buns. I hope you will keep safe; I sure miss you and worry about you. I spoke with Sarah the other day and she misses you, too. She told me that when I see you to tell you to call her. She'd love to have coffee with you."

My friend, Susan, makes ham buns and cookies every week. I go to her home each week and always pick up 20 to 30 buns and home-baked cookies. She was my go-to person for many of the years I was out there. Whenever I needed something I could not afford or get, she was always there with the solution.

I give her and the rest of her group each a gift bag and I notice the tears in Annie's eyes. I feel helpless. I want to take her away from all of this and help her to get back on her feet. I have seen other women come out of this kind of darkness and have marveled at their strength and courage. I pray that one day Annie will be able to detox once and for all. I take her in my arms and hug her and whisper to her that I will keep looking for her each Thursday. I tell her she knows where I am and that I am always here for her. I walk away, wiping away my own tears.

I do see her now and again on Thursdays and she is always with the same guy and group. I am appalled at how ill she looks. Her curls are little ringlets that hang limply. Annie always kept herself and her clothes clean, even though they were worn in places. Her hair was always brushed and those curls of hers seem to dance around her face. She often wore her little tam with a couple of curls that peaked out around the edges. I make a mental note to bring one of Gipp's baseball caps for her, as many of the men and women wear hats to protect against lice. I once was host to them after I hugged a woman living in the shelters. I felt the itch almost immediately. I got rid of them quickly, but what a horrid experience.

I am frightened for Annie and fear that one night I will learn she has died or is very ill or that no one can tell me where she is. I love her very much and always remember the sweet, gentle woman and wonderful mother she was. All I can do is keep in touch with her on the streets and give her and her group a gift bag, a sandwich, and granola bar or cookies each week I see them.

This went on for about four months and then I noticed Annie was on her own and always staying at street-link—a shelter that helped those on our streets. She seemed to be with a different guy and, at times, had bruises on her face.

This Thursday, I spot her sitting on a step.

"Hi, Annie. Oh, good grief. What happened? Who did this to you?" I sit down and take her hand in mine.

"Rick. He got some bad junk and it made him act like some madman. I couldn't stop him he was like some wild animal; I never saw him like that ever. I said something that just set him off. I don't even remember what." She is shaking and her face is messed up—bruises, black swollen eyes, her lip is twice it's normal size. Dried blood clung to the corner of her mouth. She has a purple hue to most of her face.

"Have you been to a doctor?"

"No, I'll be OK. It looks a lot worse than it is. I never seen him like this ever. I'm sure he got some bad dope."

I don't know Annie; I think you should be looked at. Let me take you to VGH emergency just to make sure you are OK. Are you hurt anywhere else?"

No, my ribs are a bit bruised from when I fell. Don't worry, Donna, I'll heal. I always do. I'll stay away from Rick for a few days till he settles down." She smiles and looks like a weird monster her lip is so swollen.

"OK, Annie. Do you want to come and stay with Gipp and me for a couple of days, just till you feel better?"

"No, I don't want to take a chance and lose my room here. Can you give me a couple of bucks so I can get something to eat?" She asks humbly. She is almost shy with me.

I am startled by her demeanor she seems embarrassed to have to ask me for money. I want to make her feel more comfortable, so I tentatively put my arm over her shoulder and give it a gentle squeeze.

"Let's go for a drive and we can go and sit down somewhere and have a proper meal. How about that? I will bring you back later. Is Rick still here?" I ask as I get up and help Annie up.

"No, he goes off for days at a time; he'll be back when he settles. I am sure he feels really, bad about what happened. He may not even remember what he did. He was pretty high and whacked out, "she says as we walk to my car.

She seems more at ease now, coming back to the Annie I remember. We drive to a small diner near the breakwater. Annie orders a burger and coffee; I do the same. We sit by a window that looks out over the ocean. Beautiful views. She seems to be waiting for me to start eating. I say a quick blessing and take a big bite out of my burger. "Yum, good burger." She bites into hers with a small dainty bite. She chews it slowly, savoring it. 'Mmm, yes. It is." She agrees. After few little bites she puts it down saying she is full. She sips her coffee. I know she has taken something; her pupils are pinpoints. We engage in small talk for some minutes, and I see she is getting antsy and jittery. I go up and pay the bill and we leave. Driving back, I notice she nods off a couple of times, snapping her head up trying to stay awake. I drop her off at her place, telling her I love her and to stay safe. I am grateful for small blessings. Just seeing her safe and even though she only ate a little, she stayed, and we chatted a little. She is still on drugs and I worry about that, but I am grateful to have had that little bit of time with her.

I feel blessed that I continue to connect with her each Thursday, and she seems to be stronger and getting healthy again. She always talks about what a great guy Rick is and how happy they are. I know she is still using, but I am delighted, that she is off the streets and in a shelter.

Annie still has bruises now and again, but she always insists it is bad drugs that set Rick off. I am not convinced but I do not want to alienate her in case she bolts or just refuses to talk to me. I keep my concerns to myself and work at eliminating the rift between us.

Once again, I lose steady contact with her and I see her sporadically. I don't know if she is still with Rick or if she has lost her permanent room or what has happened. She always tells me she is busy, or she forgot it was Thursday or some other flimsy reason why she avoids me. When I do see Annie, she is high. Then, one Thursday when I approach her, she is belligerent and walks away from me when I approach her.

She turns and assumes a combative stance and starts her rant. "I don't need to explain my actions to you or anyone else. I am my own person, and I am sick of you telling me what I should do. You don't own me! Quit following me. I do not need to see you every week and listen to same thing you preach each time is see you. Just leave me alone and get lost. I'm busy working here, trying to make some money so move on!" She spits the words at me.

I have no idea what is going on. I simply went up to her and offered her a gift bag and ask how everything was going. I stand very still and very slowly replace the gift bag into my backpack. I wait frightened to make any move toward her. I squeak when I say,

"Take good care of yourself, Annie, and please stay safe out here. I am sorry for upsetting you. Know I will carry you in my heart and prayers always." I slowly turn and walk away.

November 12, 2018

I lost touch with Annie again. I searched each week for her but to no avail.

I get a call from her on November 12; she has just been discharged from the hospital and has no place to go. She sounds very distressed; it is 10 P.M., so I go to pick her up.

"Hi, Annie. Are you OK? She is holding her tam in her hands. She is wearing a black cloth jacket that drapes just below her waist. A pink scarf is tied in a pretty knot and hangs on the outside of her jacket softening her look. She has jeans on and her usual boots. A little more worn but they look lived in and comfortable. I take the bag with her belongings and place it on the back seat of my car. You seem agitated. Jump in and if it's okay with you I can take you home with me and we talk about what is going on? I am shocked at how nervous she seems when she gets into my car.

She angrily snarls out her words.

"I have just gone through another detox hell on earth. No one cares if you have no place to go; they just tell you to leave now that you are well again. I know they need the beds but where am I supposed to go? It is cold and I have been trying to find a friend who will help me. I'm sorry to put this on you again, Donna, but you are the only person I know who is always willing to help me." She seems resentful that she had to call me for help.

I smile and tell her. "Do not apologize Annie! I am here to help it is part of my ministry. I hope you know how special you are to me and that you can call on me for help anytime. If you need a place right now you are welcome to stay with Gipp and I for a few months or until you are stronger and better able to find your own place. I haven't seen you for quite a while—tell me what's been happening. You seem pretty upset with the hospital." I feel a little awkward and am careful not to fire questions at her, after our last meeting.

She stares at her lap and mangles the tissue she is holding. "I'm not so good. Rick is threatening to kill me, and no one will help me. I went to the cops, but they just talk to him and he tells them he doesn't see me anymore. But I know he will kill me, Donna. He hates me. The last time I ran into him he called me a rat and threatened me again. He demanded every penny I owe him." As she tells me what has been happening her posture gets more aggressive.

I am dumbfounded. "What? That is appalling, Annie. Surely there is something more the police can do. Did you tell them how he beat you up when you were together?"

She goes a little more rigid. Once again, I get one of those Annie looks like, *"Really?"*

"Of course, I told them everything! She snaps. They say when they talk to him, he tells them he's never threatened me and that I am just jealous because he is with someone else. He keeps reminding me that I owe him money and if I don't pay up, he'll get his dealer to come after me. I can't pay anything right now. It's no good, Donna. I have to get out of this city. I don't know what to do. I have no money and no place to hide. I can't stay with you; he knows where you live, and he could come after me there. She pulls her scarf off and covers her face with it."

I am shocked at this astounding news. "Jeepers, Annie! Listen, I have a friend who has rooms to rent in a big place. I will phone and see if she has a room that is vacant. If she does, I'll ask her if you can stay there a couple of days while we figure out what we can do to help you out of this."

I know it is late but Bett is always up past midnight. I call her and I tell her the whole story and the threat that is hanging over Annie's head and how she has no safe place to go. She says she is happy to put Annie up for a few days and tells me to come right over.

"OK, Annie. We are going over to Bett's. She will keep you there and I will come back in the morning and we will sort this out and see what we can do to keep you safe. There is no way Rick will find you there. Hopefully, it will be for just a couple of days."

Annie is anxiously wringing her hands and wads her scarf into a tiny ball. She stays silent. I assume she is nervous of going to a stranger for help but too scared of Rick finding her to do anything else.

We drive over to Bett's.

"Hi, Bett. This is Annie. I really appreciate you helping out like this," I tell her, hugging her when she invites us in.

"No problem, Donna. Hi, Annie. Are you hungry? "she asks, taking Annie's hand in hers.

"No, I just need to sleep, I'd just like to go to bed, if that's OK with you." She is weary and apprehensive.

"OK, Annie. I'll leave you in Bett's care and I promise to call you tomorrow morning. Get a good night's sleep. I promise you are in good hands here and that we will come up with a plan tomorrow." I hug her and leave. I am sorry she is too scared to stay with Gipp and I, but I do not want to be on this guy's radar either.

The next morning, I call another friend named Betty. She comes over right away after I explain the situation. She is one of my best friends, she and Mary and I often take road trips up the island for weekends and did one to Calgary one year. Betty is a retired nurse. She is gentle and caring and will do whatever she can to help anyone in need. She has patched up the sex workers with minor cuts or bruises a time or two. She knows many of them and did an afternoon tea party for them a few months back. Over twenty showed up and we enjoyed a delightful afternoon.

We go and pick Annie up and take her for breakfast. She looks nice in a pair of black jeans and a pink sweatshirt and her one and only pair of wonderful boots. Her hair curls and nestles around her face peeping around the edges of her tam. She has obviously had a shower and maybe laundered her clothes. Whatever she and Betty got up to this morning, she looks sweet although still stressed.

"Did you sleep OK last night, Annie?" I ask.

"Yes, I slept really good. What's going to happen to me? I got nowhere to go, and I am so afraid." She whimpers. Her head in her hands. She is sitting at the table with a plate of food sitting untouched and a cup of coffee beside her plate.

"Let's not talk about it here, Annie. Betty and I are going to be with you all day and we'll work something out to keep you safe. In the meantime, eat something. You haven't touched your food you need to eat Annie."

She jumps up and glares at me.

"I'm not hungry! I just want to get out of here!" she protests.

Yikes, that startles both Betty and me! As my heartbeat slows, I quietly ask. "At least eat your toast and drink your coffee please, Annie." I beg her, hoping to settle her down. She is terrified and doesn't seem to trust we can help her.

"You will just make yourself sick if you don't eat." Betty says in her quiet voice. She puts her arm around Annie and gently eases her back on her chair. Betty sits on the chair next to her.

"Try and eat a little and we'll go for a ride and talk about a suggestion Donna and I came up with this morning Annie." Betty puts her hand over Annie's and smiles. Her voice is soft and kind.

Finally, Annie eats some toast and drinks some coffee laced with cream and gobs of sugar.

We leave Bett's and are driving around Beach Road, enjoying the November sunshine and the amazing view. The ocean is like a mirror, the calm waves gently roll in cadence to the soft breeze. The sunlight whispers over each wave, leaving its light to caress it as it disappears to unite with the sea.

"The sun always shines here for me; I will always remember that." Annie says quietly. She is more settled now that we are away from others.

I hesitantly present a solution Betty and I had decided to try when we got together this morning. "Annie, what if we could get you on a bus to Prince Albert: would you consider going there? You have family and we could contact the pastor of the Baptist church there and I know he would be willing to help you immerse yourself into the church, make new friends, and gather your family around you. Rick would have no way of knowing where you are and probably wouldn't believe you had enough money to get out of here?" I ask, hoping we can get the money to make this happen.

"I would do that," she says, listlessly. Annie is lying in the back seat of Betty's car. She is deeply depressed.

I get on the phone to our pastor and ask if he could put out a call to our congregation for a collection of funds to enable us to purchase a ticket for Annie and enough money to get her food and drink on the journey there. Amazingly, within two hours, we have enough money for the bus fare and food and two hundred dollars to spare, which she can use for miscellaneous items until she settles with her family.

We then contact the pastor at the Baptist church in Prince Albert and he promises to meet Annie at the bus station and take her to her family's home. He says he will stay in contact with her as much as she will allow and keep me informed as to how she is doing.

It is all so perfect the way everything comes together. The love of strangers reaching out to Annie, a woman none of them have met but wanted to help her in any way they could. No strings attached, just agape love. Both Betty and I are moved to tears. The day is nearly over, and we only need to make the travel arrangements, which means Annie can leave the next day.

"Annie, we're going to take you back to Bett's place now. When I get back home tonight, I'll book your trip to Prince Albert. Please make sure you are packed and ready to go before you go to bed tonight. I'll call you later and let you know what time you need to be ready in the morning. I'm not sure when the bus leaves, but we will find that out when I book it. Bett is going to have supper ready for us tonight, we'll spend this last meal together, and then Betty and I have to get home."

I am excited as I tell her this great news. She still seems lethargic and defeated, still laying on the back seat. I feel helpless and sad by what is happening to her. I know it is imperative that she gets out of Victoria and far away from Rick. I also know she has built a life here and I continue to believe she will one day be happy again. I don't know if she will get her children back, but one never knows what life holds. If she has the courage to fight her addictions and win, then I believe she could come out strong and able to care for her children again. I believe a big part of her sadness is not having custody of her children. She was such a good mom.

After enjoying a lovely supper and good conversation that Annie meekly participated in, Betty and I left for home.

The next morning, I get up and pray Annie is still willing to leave. The bus will leave at 11:30 A.M., so we don't have a lot of time to linger. I had purchased a wallet and purse for her to keep the money in, as well as some personal products like toothbrush, toothpaste, deodorant, and other things I thought she might need.

Betty picks me up at 9:30 A.M., and we drive over to get Annie.

"Hi, Bett, is Annie ready to go?" I ask as we enter her home.

"Yes, we had some breakfast and we've been just yakking away drinking coffee while we waited for you and Betty to get here. She's ready to start a new adventure, right Annie?" She takes Annie's hand and hugs it to herself; I notice the tears they both shed, and I feel miserable it has come to this.

"Well, Annie, do you feel like this is the same adventure, only in reverse?" I ask trying to keep my emotions in check, so we all don't end up blubbering our way out of here.

"Sort of. I wish I didn't have to go. I love you guys so much. I will always remember you and miss you forever," she weeps.

"Aw, c'mon Annie. Be happy. You are going home to family and childhood friends and you'll do great. You never know, you may end up back here in a couple of years. None of us know what the future holds, but you have the courage to make happen whatever path you choose. I hand her the purse with the bag of toiletries, which she puts in her small case that Bett has given her to put her few belongings in. Betty had given her a nice warm dark-blue hooded jacket earlier. She tucks that into her case too. We all hug and thank each one for everything and we step out and close the door to this part of Annie's life. We all climb into Betty's car and drive to the bus depot.

"Here's your ticket, Annie. You have enough money to see you through for a few days once you get there. Have you had a chance to call your mom and let her know you are coming?" I ask.

"Yeah, she doesn't seem too excited, but I can go there till I get a place of my own. I don't want to rely on or be a burden to my family, so I'll try and get some work right away." She says as her bottom lip starts to tremble.

She reaches out and hugs me so tight I can hardly breathe and now I lose it and start to cry. Betty embraces us both, shedding tears as well. The three of us stand huddled weeping and promising to keep in touch.

"I love you guys so much," she says as she turns and climbs on the bus. For the last time, she turns and waves goodbye to the two Bettys and me. We wave back and watch the bus pull away. We walk back to Betty's car and I weep silently as she drives me home, after dropping Bett off.

When I walk into my home, Gipp immediately comes and takes me in his arms as I sob into his chest. I am heartbroken for Annie. We both pray her life will be better in Prince Albert and that she stays off drugs and gets a good job that takes her away from the lifestyle she got immersed in here.

I heard from her along the way. The pastor in Prince Albert met her and took her home. He calls me and assures me he will stay in touch with her and keep me apprised of how she is doing.

January 2, 2019

About a month later Annie calls me.

"Hi, Donna. It's Annie. How are you doing? I miss you and the two Bettys."

"Annie, it is so good to hear your voice!" I say excitedly.

"How is everything there? Are you still at your mom's? Do you go to the church? Are you keeping in touch with the pastor? Are you working?" I blurt all these questions in my usual way. I am very, excited to hear her voice.

"Wow! Give me a minute to answer. No, I'm not at home. Me and my mom don't get along very well, so I am living with a friend. We rent this small place and it is much better for me. I'm working on the stroll again and some-times out of an agency. It's pretty good money—enough to pay my rent, food, and stuff. I don't go to church, but I talk with the pastor. He calls me a lot. He's really nice, but I don't belong in church. I'm pretty happy and I feel safe here. Thank you so much for getting me out of danger, Donna. You saved my life." She is breathless as she responds to my questions.

I laughingly reply. "No worries, Annie. I'm just grateful so many people came forward and helped to make that happen. I hope you and your mom can work through your differences. She is family, Annie, and we know how important family is. I was hoping you would get out of the sex trade and start working toward your dreams of being a photographer. I hope you still have those dreams. Are you staying clear of drugs and booze? I ask, hesitantly, as I don't want her on the defensive or to stop calling me. I hold my breath waiting for her to answer.

She sounds relaxed. "It's all OK, Donna. One day, when I have enough money saved, I will go back to school and I will buy a camera. It is still my dream. I do some drugs and drink a little, but I can control it. I need a little boost to get me through each day. I'm lonely sometimes, but the gal I live with is easy to get along with. I am slowly making friends with some of the other women. It's all good Donna. You don't need to worry about me anymore. I need to go and do some laundry, but thanks for always loving me. I'll call again soon; I don't have my own phone yet but when I do, I'll give you my number, I promise. Bye for now."

She hangs up after I tell her I love her and always and carry her in my heart, and prayers.

July 9, 2019

Annie and I keep in touch sporadically and my last conversation with her is pretty, positive. Since she went to Prince Albert, she always ends our phone conversations by telling me, "Thanks for loving me."

My phone rings early in the morning, around 10, I think. I pick it up and answer it.

"Hi, Donna. It's Annie. How are you doing?"

"Oh, Annie, it is great to hear from you. You sound good. What's happening in your life these days?" I am very, happy to hear from her.

"Nothing much. My friend and I found a sweet little house and we're having good times together. She's good to me and we both work on the same corner. I'm really happy and I have some exciting news, Donna." Her voice is shaking with excitement.

"What is it? I'm dying of curiosity Annie; spit it out," I laughingly tell her.

"I'm pregnant. I'm thrilled and so is my roommate. I can stay here, and we can both work odd shifts, so we won't need to pay a babysitter. It's a boy—I have always wanted another little boy. I know what I am going to call him." She is so excited she runs her words together.

"Wow, Annie. Is the father in the picture? Are you off all drugs? You know what horrible things the baby will go through when he is born if you take any opiates or even drink. Please tell me you are clean and sober." I probably sound aggressive to you who are reading this, but I will never forget the depth of Annie's sadness when her baby Hayley was taken away because she was born addicted. I am worried for her and the baby she is carrying.

"I have been off all drugs for four months now. I promise I will never go back down that rabbit hole again. I've got my own social worker who is helping me get all the things I will need, and she is going to work with me even after Caleb is born. It's wonderful Donna. I can't tell you how amazing my life is right now." Her joy is contagious, and I am thrilled for her.

"You sound happy, and I am proud of how you are turning your life around. We always knew you would get back on high ground, Annie. I love the name Caleb. When is your due date?"

"In three months. I hope we can get him baptized in the Baptist Church."

"In the Baptist church we dedicate babies to our Lord, I know the church will welcome Caleb on that day. Do you have all you need for when he comes home?

"Yes, people have been wonderful here. The women I work with are giving me a baby shower after he is born. I can hardly wait. I need run now Donna. I'll call again soon. Thanks for always loving me. Bye."

I laugh out loud, wow you are in a hurry to end this conversation. "Bye Annie. You are in my heart and prayers. Talk again soon." I hang up the phone and grinning from ear to ear I tell Gipp the good news.

October 15, 2019

Two months later, my phone rings, I don't remember what time of day it was. It was Pastor Tim in Prince Albert.

"Hi, Donna. I have some devastating news to tell you." He sounds grief stricken.

"What's going on?" I never thought what it was or how it could affect me. I just answered like it was common for him to call me.

"It's Annie. She was shot and killed along with her unborn baby. She was buried with him nestled in her arms yesterday; I attended the funeral." His voice trembling as he tells me about Annie.

"Oh my gosh! I haven't spoken to her for a while. I had no idea she was in danger. Why, who ... oh Lord, how can this be?" I am crying and shell shocked, running my words together, trying to get my head around this earth-shattering news.

"I don't know all the details, Donna, but I knew you needed to know. I am sorry." He sounds wounded himself.

Through my sobs I babble. "Thank you, Tim, for looking out for her and keeping me informed. I am grateful to you and I know Annie appreciated all you did for her, particularly when she first arrived. Thank you for calling me and letting me know. She was easy to love. Goodbye and thanks again." I hung up my phone, sat down, and told Gipp and we both wept, holding each other close.

Drugs

The darkness is like quicksand sucking me deep into the abyss. The abyss, at times, is a place of peace where I can wallow in the sorrow that washes over my soul and every part of my being.

Other times, the abyss is like a rushing wind that beats and batters me, tossing me against a life that I cannot pursue. Sucking all the joy and hope and leaving me exhausted and lost.

I struggle and listen to the silence around me, hoping I can reach a thread of life that I can cling to. The world is not my friend. The darkness washes over my thoughts and the noise of silence shatters my hope.

I know I am a mother, a friend, a human. I am shattered into few pieces that I must glue back together. I need to feel the softness of the drug as it eases me into a peaceful sleep. Escape is my world. I no longer can reach outside the fog that clutters my brain.

I have become an invisible interloper to my friends, my children, and any who cared. I live on the dark side.

I embrace the enclosed closet where my life hangs in the balance of desire to cling to what once was and the fight to hang on to the now.

I will not ask you to understand, because I cannot understand. The path I choose I chose not willingly and yet I know it is my choice but not. The drug is my enemy and my ally. I am at peace when I embrace its warmth. I am in turmoil when it no longer infuses its warmth.

I am me and yet not. I am lost to the light and nestle in the inhumanity of counterfeit love. The drugs keep me in the warmth of nothing. I am invisible and no longer viable to any who once cherished me.

And so, I choose the forbidden void; it is my shield, my safe place, a place to hide my soul forever.

I no longer want to be found. The break is complete. I am me, not the me you once knew and loved. I am a flicker living in a lost expanse.

I wrote following poem, trying to explain how I believe life can take us down some very crooked roads. Maybe Annie's road. I believe that at the end of the road, God is there to embrace us.

Me

Some souls are born broken.

Cast on the shores of life,

To find a place to be,

To run, to laugh, and to play.

But at times, just to weep,

Lost in the cesspool of darkness.

Struggling to find the light,

But never quite able to capture it.

Elusive and wandering,

It lights the path of those

Who seek to destroy.

What little space the soul has found.

Each shattered piece finding

A small piece of life.

Always looking for

That someone to watch,

And care enough

To make a whole person,

From all the little pieces.

But some things are never meant to be.

So, each piece finds its own light.

The whole lost to time and chance.

But I must believe that one day

My God will knit together

That which life has shattered.

And hold them next to His heart

And whisper in their ear.

I love you.

You have always been mine.

Epilogue

I am trying to put together words to tie up this story. I have shed many tears writing it when the memories flood and shatter my heart again. I urge any of you who read this to understand the how and whys we make the choices that lead to devastation. Chance and circumstance are bedfellows—no one knows where life will lead us, or how it will end. I digress here to try and explain how I struggled with this situation. I remember being disappointed in myself in not seeing what was really happening. I was convinced that Len was the villain, and I was determined to persuade Annie to get him out of her life. I was blinded to how Annie was using drugs to cope with life. There is no doubt in my mind that Len had to get out of her life. This point in my walk with Annie, I was still convinced that was necessary for her to be able to stay clean and sober.

I can remember thinking back to when I first met her and how she was positive and happy. She would always start our conversations with, "The sun is shining again today, Donna. It always shines here for me each day!" She was coping well with her move from Prince Albert. Her children were clean, well fed, and deeply loved and cared for.

I tried to remember when I noticed Annie using, but could not be certain because at times it seemed more like she was depressed, and sadness was what I was seeing. But I knew better. I should have confronted her right at the start when I noticed her drug use accelerating. I knew it wasn't up to me to make her stop, but because of the ministry I do, it is on me to talk about what I see. To offer my help to her in whatever capacity I can. Hindsight is great, but the guilt I felt was almost overpowering. I even thought about just staying out of her life and not including her in my Thursday night ministry. My heart simply, wouldn't let me walk away from Annie and her children, no matter where the journey took us. I know Len resented my interference. He knew I would do everything in my power to see that Annie kept custody of their children.

Some of you reading this book might judge both Sarah and me for sticking our noses in where it didn't belong. We watched her struggle and connive, and do whatever she had to do to balance all the negative vibes Len brought into the equation with the positive vibes he gave to their children. It was always nerve-wracking for me when the phone rang in the middle of the night or days Annie called in tears.

-0-

CPSIA information can be obtained
at www.ICGtesting.com
Printed in the USA
BVHW091944050422
633362BV00001B/17